SOUTHERNERS

OXMOOR HOUSE
BIRMINGHAM ALABAMA

SOUTHERNERS
PORTRAIT OF A PEOPLE

CHARLES KURALT
WITH IRWIN GLUSKER

SOUTHERNERS
PORTRAIT OF A PEOPLE

Copyright 1986 by Oxmoor House, Inc.
Book Division of Southern Progress Corporation
P.O. Box 2463, Birmingham, Alabama 35201

Library of Congress Catalog Number: 85-52363
ISBN: 0-8487-0690-0
Manufactured in the United States of America

Southerners: Portrait of a People
originated with Irwin Glusker and was
developed for publication jointly by
Oxmoor House, Inc. and The Glusker Group, Inc.

For Oxmoor House, Inc.

Editor: Rebecca Brennan
Writer-Researcher: Mark Childress
Editorial Assistant: Lenda Wyatt
Production Manager: Jerry Higdon
Associate Production Manager: Rick Litton

For The Glusker Group, Inc.

Editorial Director: Irwin Glusker
Project Manager: Alicia Hathaway
Assistant Project Manager: Christina Boufis
Layout: Christian von Rosenvinge
Contributing Editor: Elizabeth Pearce
Research Staff: Meryle Evans, Philip Napoli,
                Melissa McRaney

FOREWORD

Don't mistake me.

I love the flinty hills of old New England and those angular, laconic, economic people, who never use two words when one will do, or spend two dollars for a thing worth fifty cents.

I love the Great Plains, where the flat fields of winter wheat stretch out to the flat horizon, and sturdy, dusty men wearing seed company caps lift a finger of greeting from the steering wheels of their tractors when you meet them on the section roads.

I love the mountain West for its purity and its trout rivers tumbling and its storm clouds building among the peaks and its white-faced cattle grazing in the broad valleys with their rumps to the wind, and for the horseman on the rise, cowboy hat shading his eyes, the romantic, sunburnt survivor.

I love the cliffs the Pacific Ocean breaks against, and the people who live on the land behind the cliffs in a New America of their own devising. The whole, bright land attracts me and amazes me.

But this book is about Home.

In the South, the breeze blows softer than elsewhere through the pine trees, and accents fall softer on the ear. Neighbors are friendlier, and nosier, and more talkative. (By contrast with the Yankee, the Southerner never uses one word when ten or twenty will do.) The spring is prettier, the summer hotter and happier, the fall longer and sadder, the winter shorter than elsewhere on the continent. This is a different place. Our way of thinking is different, as are our ways of seeing, laughing, singing, eating, meeting and parting. Our walk is different, as the old song goes, our talk and our names. Nothing about us is quite the same as in the country to the north and west.

What we carry in our memories is different, too, and that may explain everything else. In this book, above all, I have tried to put down what we carry in our memories.

Charles Kuralt

ONE

They say the South is at last entering the mainstream. Well, as somebody pointed out, one-third of Americans call themselves Southerners. That *is* a mainstream.

There's no doubt in anyone's mind that people born and brought up in Georgia, in Mississippi, in Alabama, in Louisiana, Florida, Tennessee, Kentucky, Virginia, Arkansas, North Carolina, or South Carolina are Southerners and always have been. They are tied together by strong bonds of family, land, language, and history.

But there are so many different kinds of Southerners. Where do you draw the lines? Is a Texan a Southerner? If he hails from east of the Pecos, he surely is. Are you a Yankee if you happen to live across the Missouri state line, even if you love grits and turnip greens? You're not. Do we count people in Maryland, who speak like Southerners, but whose forebears gave a frosty reception to Robert E. Lee? We do.

We should also speak of West Virginians as Southerners, assuredly, even though that state was created by Abraham Lincoln after the people within its boundaries sided with him against the Confederacy.

If we measured Southerners by the standard of who stood with whom in a war now over a hundred years gone, of course, hardly anybody in the western part of North Carolina would be considered a Southerner. In those parts, as in sections of Tennessee and Alabama—and most of the border states as well—most people were Republicans, and for Lincoln, and opposed to the Civil War. Up there in those hollows, people thought quite rightly that the war was a terrible waste.

But an afternoon's drive out from Asheville into those very hills will convince you in some indefinable way that you're in a Southern land, among Southerners.

It is worth noting that people in extreme southern Illinois have always considered themselves Southerners, in spite of their place on the map. They *act* Southern. Their sympathies were with the South in the Civil War. They farmed as Southerners. All of the people they traded with were Southerners. They felt themselves much closer to the South than to, say, Chicago or Gary. To this day, Cairo, Illinois, is as Southern a town as you would ever wish to visit.

And you do find Southerners in Missouri—not Southerners just by virtue

'Penny Portraits' fill the window of a photographer's studio in Birmingham, Alabama. Photographed by Walker Evans in 1936.

of the fact that they came from the South or their folks happened to come from the South. They *feel* Southern.

I guess a Southerner is just anybody who says he is.

You don't find as many introspective, lonesome people down here. The Southerner is independent minded and democratic and feels he is equal to any other person. And in the Tidewater areas, the Delta of Mississippi, and parts of Virginia, he feels he is perhaps slightly superior.

Margaret Mitchell wrote an enormous (and enormously successful) novel of longing and nostalgia for that South, long after it was, as she put it, gone with the wind. She captured the popular imagination with a portrait of the vanished Southern aristocracy as mystically righteous, religiously genteel, tragically doomed from the start. Her tale is as well established in the American mind today as the legends of King Arthur in the British mind, but it's also about as well grounded in fact.

To me, it was a Northerner—Stephen Vincent Benét in *John Brown's Body*—who best characterized that particular South: the magnolia-scented, pride-of-clan, quick-to-anger, neo-medieval region of the feudal Southern lord.

> Bury the bygone South.
> Bury the minstrel with the honey-mouth,
> Bury the broadsword virtues of the clan,
> Bury the unmachined, the planters' pride,
> The courtesy and the bitter arrogance,
> The pistol-hearted horsemen who could ride
> Like jolly centaurs under the hot stars.
> Bury the whip, bury the branding-bars,
> Bury the unjust thing
> That some tamed into mercy, being wise,
> But could not starve the tiger from its eyes
> Or make it feed where beasts of mercy feed.
> Bury the fiddle-music and the dance,
> The sick magnolias of the false romance
> And all the chivalry that went to seed
> Before its ripening.

When he describes that South, which was so fatally flawed by its casual cruelty to blacks, Benét is writing about a place no living Southerner remembers, and a society most Southerners who lived at the time were not part of.

The Tidewater man, the aristocrat, isn't exactly the man I'm thinking of. Not the plantation owner, or the proprietor of a large farm, or the Virginian proud of his ancestors. He's there, all right, in our history, but I never knew him.

It's the Anglo-Saxon, Scotch-Irish settler who is to me the characteristic Southerner, or the black tenant farmer hoping things would be better for the children, the farmer, the fisherman, the man who lived off what the land provided—and who thus grew close to the land.

There was always truth in the expression "Southern hospitality," and

Floyd Burroughs, a cotton sharecropper of Hale County, Alabama, photographed in the summer of 1936 by Walker Evans.

9

there still is. People down here are more open to outsiders. They trust you until they see some reason not to.

Recognizing that it certainly isn't true of all of us, I would propose that a Southerner is distinguished by a sense of neighborliness; a garrulous quality, a wish to get together a lot. As you look through these pictures, you'll notice that we've always found plenty of excuses for getting together—barbecues and fish fries and quilting bees and corn shuckings and camp meetings and barn dances.

The South was always such a rural society that those social events were the only times people had a chance to rub elbows, swap gossip, exchange information on crops. And it seems to me that at least a remnant of that ancient conviviality still characterizes us in the South of today.

This Southerner we've been talking about—the one who so enjoys the company of others—is not a mountain man. The mountain people do have more reticence toward strangers. They're really the same people, the same old Scotch-Irish stock, so their insularity must be a reflection of their landscape, the hills and hollows, with no horizons. It's only when you get beneath his reserve that the mountaineer's great ability as a storyteller comes out.

Land, and the landscape, are critical to how we place ourselves as Southerners, but they are not the only determinants. Within a mile of each other, in the Low Country of South Carolina, you'll find a plantation owner and a black Geechee woman. Two more different individuals do not exist on the earth.

But certain people tend to be proud because of the land they live on: the South Carolinian, for example—not just the Charlestonian aristocracy—but the South Carolinian in general. And the Virginian, of course, is the one who is so family and history proud. That comes from Jefferson and Madison and Washington, from having all those great men to reflect on.

Most of these people are related in some way to somebody—they had an uncle who was a judge in the courthouse that Jefferson was the architect of, or some other tenuous connection to the past. Most of the rest of the South doesn't have anywhere near so much to be proud of—plenty of history, to be sure, but not of that nation-building kind.

For most people in the South, history is contained in our families. With the exception of major events that resounded all the way out in the countryside, much of history has marched past the Southerner without his even being aware of it. When you live, as many of us have, miles from the nearest town, and perhaps even more miles from the nearest newspaper or telegraph office, far-off events lose their importance. What's important is what happens where you live, to the people you know.

Even if the family's not a distinguished one—even if it's entirely undistinguished by the standards of outsiders—Southerners are interested in their families. There's much talk about whose boy managed to buy some land, about whose daughter went to school and got to be a nurse.

This intense preoccupation with the family, coupled with the famous Scotch-Irish quick temper, has often produced uncomfortable results. In the

The Bruce Dudley family of Louisville visiting Stephen Foster's "Old Kentucky Home," in Bardstown, Kentucky, circa 1935.

*Overleaf:
A gathering in Gordon County, Georgia, in the late 1800s.*

11

North, you're apt to get mugged by somebody who doesn't even know you. In the South, that would almost never happen. Violence down here has rarely been directed at strangers. If your life is in danger here, it's from your own cousin, or your wife. It's *family*. All of that dueling nonsense that went on has been consigned to history, but today it takes the form of switchblade knives in a card game, or just two friends who get drunk and fall to arguing, and one of them shoots the other.

There exists nowhere else that I know of that eagerness to do violence, and then perhaps patch it up the next day. The family feud, I think, has been much overdone; at least I never saw any evidence of it. I'm sure it did exist among certain isolated mountain families. But in most of the South it was your own family you were fighting, and you were apt to say the next day, "God, I must have been terrible drunk. I'm sorry."

This, of course, was while you were visiting the poor fellow in the hospital.

These, then, are things that occasionally divided us, but more often were our common ground: a love of togetherness, of land, and of family; a shared language, with endless stories to be told in any one of a variety of accents and then passed by the next generation; a curious relationship to history, threaded through with our propensity for sudden violence.

In my experience, the Southerner knows who he is and where he came from. These things are one and the same. I know that my life has gone the way it has because I came from a certain people, from a place, that I'll never forget. Let me tell something about it.

I was born in North Carolina, and although my family lived all over the South while I was growing up, North Carolina was home. My father was a Massachusetts man who had come down to Chapel Hill because he got a scholarship in geology. My mother was a beautiful young schoolteacher from Onslow County, near the coast (where Camp Lejeune is today).

We visited the Massachusetts side of the family, but life was in North Carolina.

The Great Depression was upon us, and my father found there was no call for geologists. So after working at a series of very menial jobs—creosoting telephone poles, things like that—he decided he would go back and study social work, because it appeared to him that was going to be the booming occupation of the time. Of course, it was.

My first memory is of a little town called Stedman, a crossroads near Fayetteville. My mother taught school there while my father was back at Chapel Hill. We had a black housekeeper named Rosa, whom I loved as much as my mother. Rosa took care of me when my mother was off teaching. We could see the school from the house, and we'd watch together for my mother to come home. It's Rosa I remember most clearly from that time. She made apple butter that I lived for. I could eat bowls and bowls of it, and did.

Then we lived in Washington, North Carolina, the *original* Washington of this country, a small city on the Pamlico River. I started school there. By the time I was in the third grade, I was much more urbane. I was becoming interested in comic books and adventure.

Playing cowboys and Indians, we used to ride broomsticks for

Selected as Master Farmer
for 1937 by Progressive
Farmer magazine, J. R. Miller
of Sylvester, Georgia,
sits for a formal portrait
with Mrs. Miller.

horses—except for one kid, named Charles, who actually had a horse.
A *white* horse! He lived in a big house on the Pamlico. We hated him with the pure hatred that is born of burning envy.

One time, we secretly made a raft. (I know I hadn't read *Huckleberry Finn* yet, but perhaps someone in our group had.) We found a part of a raft that had landed on the riverbank, and we improved it so we could get out on the river.

All of us kept the secret, as if it were sacred. One day we actually floated on the river, about a hundred yards I guess, and decided among ourselves, "Okay, the thing works, now we're really going to take a trip." We weren't going to go to New Orleans, but we were going at least as far as the railroad bridge.

But Charles, the one with the horse, whom we had excluded, was a sensible boy. Because he thought it was dangerous, he told on us. Our parents came down on us in alarm. That was a disaster. We all ended up wishing we'd never thought of building a raft.

I suppose that if we'd really set out on that trip, things might have worked out as they did for Huck. We'd surely have wound up in some different place.

Our family moved to Birmingham, to Atlanta for a while, and then back to Charlotte by the time I was eleven. But all that time, I knew I had a home. Whenever there came a chance for us all to go back to my grandparents' place, my mother's old home place in Onslow County, we would go.

It is that farm I remember best of all.

It was a prosperous farm, in Carolina tobacco country terms, and we certainly weren't poor by the standard of the day. But it was a farm with no electricity or machinery or indoor plumbing. It's odd, because I was only four or five when I first saw it and never saw it again after my grandfather's death, but I remember every single thing about that place. I can see it now. A hundred-acre tobacco farm. A two-story house. A front lawn that wasn't much of a lawn, mostly sand. The side yard was too well shaded by sycamore trees to have any grass. There were chickens underfoot. Two mules, two cows, two pigs. A tobacco barn down the road, which you couldn't see from the house. A corncrib, a barn with a wagon inside, a hayloft above. A picket fence, whitewashed once upon a time.

We moved the wagon out of the barn when my Aunt Trixie came home from teaching school with her first car, a Chevrolet, which needed to be parked under cover, of course. Trixie had just managed to afford a car. So the old farm wagon got parked in the yard near the house, after that.

It was an old house. It had been in the family a hundred years, I suppose, built by my grandmother's forebears. There was an addition, formal front rooms, which were themselves built well before the turn of the century. My grandfather had a great big toolbox in the shade on the back porch. There was a pump back there, where you got water for the house. I remember the houseflies out there by the hundreds. My grandfather would do many of his chores there—fitting a new axe handle to an old axe—while he was sitting on that toolbox. He was very satisfied to sit on that toolbox and work at whatever he had to do.

My grandfather certainly never went to college, perhaps never even to high school. In his youth, he had been a fisherman down there on the coast, and so he was to me a kind of romantic character. He told stories about storms at sea and shipmates swept overboard.

And he was contrary. He wouldn't go to church, didn't have any interest in it at all. (My grandmother went, of course, for the social reasons.) He did have a suit that he could wear to church, but he hated wearing it. He was comfortable in his overalls, comfortable sitting with his back up against one of those sycamore trees. He would have a big bucket of oysters, and he'd sit right on the ground, which of course was beneath the dignity of all the women in the family. He'd just sit there in his overalls, with his bucket of oysters and an oyster knife. He'd reach in, open one, pop it in his mouth, and toss the shell on the ground. This was awesome to me. I remember thinking that was a real man, someone who could sit there and eat those things.

That was a happy half hour for him. I can see his white moustaches drooping down and that old Anglo-Saxon face that we all know—the one that Dorothea Lange photographed.

It was certainly the women who were the strong ones in the family. My grandmother, really, in my memory and the memory of many other people, was saintly. She had a gentle face. In the years I knew her, she wore her hair in a bun, tied up behind her head. She was endlessly patient. She was well educated; she was herself a teacher. And a reader, which was rare in that community. She wasn't sanctimonious about it. She just liked books. She taught a lot of children to read, I think, both in and out of schools.

She was kind, and worked terribly hard, as Southern women did. I remember her washing the laundry in the yard, in a big black pot with a fire under it. She would stir the mess of lye soap and overalls and long johns with a hoe handle—none of which suited her. She was not an elegant lady, or anything like that; she was a hardworking woman all of her life. But it was a pity, it seems to me now, that she had to work so hard at cooking and stirring the clothes instead of having a chance to do what she really wanted to do—read and teach.

My grandfather had rigged a swing for me in one of the sycamores in the front yard, and I used to swing there. Or run wild in the orchard, among the twisted-up old apple trees. Nobody ever seemed to pick the apples. They fell and rotted on the ground. Perhaps somebody did pick them and make pies out of them, but my memory is the pungent apple smell from the apples on the ground.

The farm was six or eight miles from town, and then another mile down a hot sandy road—very hot, I remember, because if you were barefoot you couldn't stand it. You had to find shade to walk in. This was white sand, and I don't care how tough you were, you couldn't walk on it. In the grass there were sandspurs. You always were barefoot, and always stepped on sandspurs, and it always hurt like hell.

In the evenings, the grown-ups sat on the front porch. That's the only use I ever remember for the porch; it was for sitting in the dark at night. To get there, you didn't walk through the house, through the parlor and all that. Nobody ever walked through the parlor, or thought much about that part

When it's apple-blossom time in central Virginia . . . photo late 1800s.

19

of the house. You went out and walked around the house from the back.

You could count after the lightning flashes—one one thousand, two one thousand—to tell how many miles away the lightning was. I remember chasing the lightning bugs and putting them in a jar with holes in the top. June bugs, you would catch if you could, tie a string to one of their legs, and let them fly around at the end of the string. I don't remember what you did with them after you tired of that.

But there was always the porch swing. I loved sitting there after dark, curled up, with my grandmother or someone else, and listening to the talk.

In the side yard there was a bell, never rung. My grandmother told me that in the old days, when she was young, they would ring the bell at all mealtimes. Not to summon hands in from the fields, because there were none. But to signal to anybody who heard the bell as he passed by on the road that he was welcome to come in and eat.

If someone came, she said, it was considered impolite even to ask his name, or to ask him questions about himself. If he were a polite person, of course, he'd introduce himself, but if he didn't—feed him anyway.

That's what a Southerner was.

The front door was never used. If anyone had ever come to the front door, the dogs would have run under the bed. The front rooms were never used, except for funerals, and weddings, and Christmas. All of life went on in the fields, in the yard, on the porch, in the back of the house at the wood stove, where my grandmother cooked the best food I can remember. Clabber biscuits, which were better, I am certain, because they were cooked in the wood stove.

She cooked always. The meals were whatever was growing at the time, and that included corn, black-eyed peas, beets, beans, cabbages, collards, and turnip greens. There was a pantry absolutely full of food in mason jars. Everything that could be grown was put up for the winter. There was everything in that pantry, and the best of all were the spiced peaches.

Whatever was left over from dinner would still be on the table at breakfast, so it was not unusual to have black-eyed peas with your eggs and grits in the morning. The food was magnificent. They never cooked vegetables without salt pork, to give them a little taste.

Hog-slaughtering day was the day that persuaded me never to be a farmer. I hated all the squealing and blood. But I loved all the good things that followed, especially the hams. There was a smokehouse full of country hams, which smelled moldy and hammy and briny. My grandfather was really good at making hams, famous for it in that part of the country.

I don't know how old I was when I had my first hamburger. We never had beef. We had pork and chicken; the cow was for milk. Chicken, especially on Sunday. An old hen who'd stopped laying would get her head chopped off for Sunday dinner. And Sunday dinner was always—different, though it wasn't necessarily better. It was served in the dining room.

We ate all other meals in the kitchen. The meals were at six in the morning, twelve noon, and six in the evening; breakfast, dinner, and supper. You could always count on having your meals on time.

Nobody ever came close to being hungry.

Members of the Home Demonstration Club display homemade cheeses in Madison County, Virginia, 1939.

The arrival of the Sears, Roebuck catalog was always a big event. I remember the thrill of looking through it. I tried not to let anybody catch me studying the pictures of actual women in their underwear.

There was a good deal of dreaming with these catalogs, but very little ordering. The catalog was a wish book, but it was useful in other ways: when we were done wishing, we used the old catalogs in the outhouse.

I don't remember ever going to the store to buy anything more than an Orange Crush. There was a store out on the highway, and we would go there sometimes, but it was always for a treat, and the treat for me was always the same—an Orange Crush in a ribbed bottle.

They didn't buy many things. They didn't have to. All they bought was what they absolutely had to spend money for, and they hated to spend money. They bought maybe salt, flour, cornmeal, and Postum, which is what they drank. Everything else came from the farm. Once upon a time, they had even fashioned clothing there. There was a loom, where my grandmother had made the cloth. Somebody was always cutting out a new blouse from a Simplicity pattern, and there was sometimes a quilt in progress.

When it's really cold, and you're in a feather bed, with your grandmother's quilts weighting you down—well, there's no place like that on this earth.

There was no Camp Lejeune then, only a little Marine outpost called Tent Camp. I used to walk there, pulling an old red wagon loaded with milk and sugar cookies that my grandmother had made for me to go sell to the marines. I don't remember ever getting any money—perhaps I did—but mainly what I got were globes and anchors and sharpshooter medals. Great stuff like that. They would say, "Give me a bunch of cookies, and I'll give you a medal."

I probably don't have all the details right. If my grandmother were alive, you can bet she would be correcting me right now.

There were Venus flytraps in the woods, those amazing plants that digest insects. A fly flies in, and the trap closes. Something about the plant makes it close when its little hairs are tickled. I used to go through the woods, endlessly tickling Venus flytraps with a straw to watch them close. I presumed they were there for the purpose of being tickled shut by little boys.

I was told never to go into the woods behind the house. There was a logging road there, and snakes.

I was out at the woodpile one night, where I'd gone to get kindling wood. I was in the dark, and something slapped me in the leg. I thought I'd stepped on a piece of wood, but I'd been bitten by a rattlesnake.

My grandmother cured me. She did what was the accepted therapy of the day: take a paring knife, make the cut bleed, suck out some of the poison.

My leg swelled up twice its size, and ached terribly. But there was something manly about having been bitten by a rattlesnake when you were six years old—and having survived to tell the tale.

My grandparents were humane for that time and place, and decent. They never said the word "nigger," or anything bad about black people. If I came home repeating some racial slur, my grandmother would speak to

Walter Duplantis and his daughter Clara Ann at watermelon on the steps of a store near Houma, Louisiana, 1947.

23

me sharply about that. If someone visiting used that word, she corrected them, even if they were her friends.

Above all, we children were not to behave like poor whites. We were always to be dignified and polite. We were to call our elders "Mr." and "Mrs." whether they were black or white, and stand when we were introduced.

I can't say that I was actually conscious of class then. I knew we were better off than some. Our nearest neighbor was a poor black family, and I went over there a lot. I had a friend there, an older boy whose name was Buck.

When I was five, I got a bicycle for Christmas, which was the greatest present I ever received. I couldn't believe it. An actual bicycle! But I didn't know how to ride it. Buck was glad to come teach me to ride the bicycle, because he had never had one either. It was really a chance for him to ride mine. I learned to ride by more or less watching Buck struggling with the bike in the soft sand in front of the house. Buck would spend half an hour showing me how, then let me ride for five minutes. I finally figured out what he was doing, and resented it (though I was grateful for the instruction).

Buck's mother was nice to me. She never failed to invite me to stay if mealtime came around when I was at their house. (I often contrived to be there about then.) And I would stay to eat her delicious ham biscuits.

My grandmother would feed Buck, too, but not at the table. She'd hand us the biscuits out the door, and we'd eat on the porch. I suppose Buck knew he couldn't sit at the table, and I never thought about it. Racial discrimination was just part of everyday life, part and parcel with pellagra and tar-paper shacks—things nobody misses now.

Death was a part of life, in the South. My mother's two sisters, Betty and Trixie, both died of tuberculosis. My mother, the youngest of the three, was the sole survivor. I remember Trixie's slow death. She lay dying for months and months, and I puzzled over it. I didn't understand death. Still don't, I guess. But the people of the community gathered around us, and Trixie was buried in the graveyard where I might be buried someday, down there in Onslow County. There's a move afoot now in my family to fix up the graveyard, and I'm glad.

Funerals were very cooperative things. Nobody would think of being left out of a funeral. And church, of course, was a social event. Some of the people in that county would walk to wherever there was a preaching. People went great distances to get to church, and I don't believe it had so much to do with religious fervor as with a chance to see other people.

Sometimes, now, on Sunday in the South, I see people coming out of church, or getting ready to go in, especially out in the country. They stand around outside for an hour after church, even if there's no dinner-on-the-grounds, or anything like that. Black churches are even more that way—folks get dressed up in their very best for the one day, and stand around and talk and talk. You don't see that so much in the North. When church is over up there, people go home.

There really weren't many churches in the South until the great Baptist religious revival in the 1830s. When William Byrd, the Virginia aristocrat, came through the South, he couldn't find churches anywhere until

*Children dressed for
Sunday school,
near Hampton, Virginia,
1899.*

he got to Charleston. In the town of Edenton, then the capital of North Carolina, he didn't find a one. In his travels through North Carolina, Byrd remarked, "I believe this is the only metropolis in the Christian or Mahometan world where there is neither church, chapel, mosque, synagogue, or any other place of worship of any sect or religion whatsoever." It wasn't until the circuit-riding Baptist ministers came along that churches sprang up in the countryside.

But when it got going, it really got going. Today, some of the big-city churches are enormous institutions, and powerful, of course. William Byrd, the austere Anglican, would be amazed by the power of the Baptists.

Of course to me there was no event in the South so joyous as a church supper or a dinner-on-the-grounds, because it really was a bringing-together of the whole community. Women would always get together for just visiting, but usually that took place on Sunday too, because they were too busy working during the week.

I am only a little past fifty, and I have a memory of what was really a primitive farm. There wasn't any electricity, nor any machinery of any kind. Today you can't imagine a farm without machinery, but the most sophisticated machine on my grandparents' farm was probably the disc harrow that was pulled by the mule.

I remember riding the mule bareback—I guess they were indulging me because I was a little boy, but at the time I thought I was helping.

To plow, you walked behind the plow, and the mule. I could do that by the time I was six. The mule knew the route so well that I just walked behind, and he knew what to do. He'd turn around at the end of the row, and come back.

There was a lot of working together. The neighbors would come and help you string your tobacco and hang it in the barn for curing; then you would go down the road and help them with theirs. They would come from all the other farms, and make a day of it. I was a hander. I would take five or six leaves—I forget—and hand to an experienced stringer, who would take them, make a twist with the tobacco twine around the stick, then with his other hand reach for another handful of tobacco, so that he would end up with the tobacco hanging neatly from both sides of the stick. Then that would hang in the barn.

These were barns made of logs, squared off, chinked with mud, and heated by wood fires in mud kilns. The trick was to keep the heat even, to cure the tobacco evenly. Because I liked to, my grandfather would invite me to pull the thermometer on a pulley on a string up to the little mica window, to be sure the heat was staying even.

My grandmother used to tell me about market day. They would take the tobacco to market—in our case to Kinston, the market my grandfather preferred because he felt he got a little better price in Kinston.

Then there was the ritual of the auctioneer stopping at each pile of tobacco, and he'd stop at your pile, and there would follow this little ten- or fifteen-second auction. He'd reach down under to make sure the bottom leaves were as good quality as the ones on top. (In my grandfather's case, they were. He was a quality tobacco raiser, he felt.) They'd have that brief auction,

Several generations at work in S. G. Gibson's tobacco field in Charlton County, Georgia, 1929.

27

and right there on the spot, the auctioneer would pay in cash. And that would be all the money the family would see that year. That was it. For the year. Fifteen seconds. I don't know how much money it would have been.

My grandmother would take a little of it and go buy a dress, and maybe a hat. And my grandfather would take his little bit of it and go out with the other men and drink. I never knew him to drink any other time; alcohol was a luxury that nobody could afford. But I remember usually on market day he was sort of . . . carried home. And then the next morning he was ready to go for another year, without any more indulgences of any kind.

I remember my grandmother's tales about the days when coming home from market was dangerous because there were bandits along the road, or highwaymen as she called them, who would rob you and take all your money. So somebody literally rode shotgun. You never came back from market day without somebody up in the front, bearing a gun.

Admittedly, that was a story she told me when I was a little boy, but it says something about how close we are to the days when the South was lawless and wild.

One day soon, I suppose, the little farmer will be gone. There will be enormous farms run mostly by machinery, irrigation machines, combines. Perhaps the little farmer with his hundred acres and his mule didn't have much chance against such a future anyway, but at least he could feed his family. He didn't expect to get rich.

Ordinarily, he didn't borrow against his harvest. He didn't borrow at all from a bank. His whole purpose was to make enough money from his crops to buy enough seed for next year, and to be sure his family was fed. He lived outside the money economy. He thought in terms of his pigs having pigs, and his milk cow having a calf so that he would have another milk cow. There were no balance sheets, because there was no money to speak of.

Today, the purpose of agribusiness is to turn a profit. But that farmer rarely ended the year with any more than he had the year before. It would be nice if he did, but if he wound up with a new dress for his wife and a couple of extra presents at Christmastime, he had done well.

I'll always be glad that I remember that farm, because it gives me an understanding of how life was.

I wouldn't let my child do it today, at that age, but back in the forties when I was a teenager, my folks didn't see anything wrong with letting me hitchhike around the country, to see something of it. I intended one year to go as far as California, but I never got any farther west than Wisconsin. I will never forget the first time I saw a Wisconsin dairy farm—the look of it! The black earth, the green meadows. I had never seen anything like that. I hadn't imagined that farms could look so prosperous—the tidy dairy barns, everything so pretty and perfect. I thought, holy smoke! These people must be rich!

Of course, in the South we just weren't used to it. We had gullies and broomstraw, and the barn was apt not to be painted, so the Southern farm was not typically what you would call a thing of beauty. It was utilitarian in every way, no wasted motion, because the farmer was so busy that he didn't have time to paint the barn and make the place look nice, though his wife

Originally introduced to control erosion and to feed livestock, kudzu became the South's "green outlaw." At left, a unique barn built for curing kudzu hay on the farm of Seth P. Starrs in Alabama in the 1930s.

might plant some petunias in an old tire by the road, to try to dress the place up a little bit.

A mountain man in North Carolina once told me, "Oh, yes! This is good strong land we have around here. It has to be, to hold up all the rocks." All you could do, if you had a poor farm, was to make a joke about it—and to get out of it what you could.

And it's true that the Southern farmer had a harder row to hoe. The Southern farmer wasn't a particularly productive one, compared to farmers in other regions. He generally didn't have good land to work with, unless he owned a stretch of river bottom. By and large he was working with sandy soil or with red clay, and doing the best he could.

All word from the outside world came in the mail. The Raleigh *News and Observer*, the *National Geographic*, and the *Progressive Farmer* all came in the mail. I'm sure the *Geographic* subscription was a luxury, but the Raleigh paper and the *Progressive Farmer* seemed necessities, to me.

It's no coincidence that the *Progressive Farmer* and progressive farming came along at the same time. Progressive is not a word you would think of to describe most Southern farmers, but they became more so, thanks to that magazine.

If he could read, the farmer could find in Clarence Poe's magazine new ideas for making his farm better: how to contour his rows so the erosion wouldn't be so bad in the spring, or how it was worth it to go ahead and spend the money on fertilizer, though he had never thought so.

This coincided with all those Roosevelt programs aimed at giving the farmer a little help. At last there was a county agent to show him ways to get more out of his soil.

So times changed, and mostly for the better. I remember the first time I saw my grandmother cry. She was standing at the end of the sand road, and wiping her eyes with her apron. It was not anything alarming; they were tears of joy. She could see the rural electrification truck, the REA light poles coming up the road to electrify the farm.

From then on, we had a light bulb hanging over the kitchen table. From then on, that county always voted Democratic, because they remembered Franklin Roosevelt brought them the light.

And what that meant, the reason my grandmother wept, was not only that she didn't have to pump the water from the pump on the porch anymore, or go to the well. It meant entering modern life.

Winter on a farm in Logan County, Kentucky, 1978. A boy does a balancing act while on his morning round.

Left: A member of the Missouri National Guard, Harry Truman, our thirty-third president, served as a World War I officer.

Above: North Carolinian Andrew Johnson, successor to Lincoln, was the only president to be impeached. He was later acquitted.

Right: The legacy of Thomas Jefferson includes the Declaration of Independence and the University of Virginia.

Above left: John Tyler of Virginia became the country's tenth president, after Harrison's untimely death.

Above: Fellow Virginian James Madison watched the White House burn during the War of 1812.

Left: Georgian Jimmy Carter's brand of politics combined idealism with evangelical fervor.

Above: James Knox Polk North Carolina is flanked by wife, Sarah, at his right and former First Lady Dolley Madison at his left.

Right: Texan Lyndon Johnson, always a little larger than life, rides tall the saddle.

Below: Born in South Carolina, "Old Hickory," Andrew Jackson, was our first Populist president.

What is it about a region that produces great leaders? The South, especially in our nation's earliest days, produced many of the fine men who led the country with wisdom and vision. Virginia, which still prides itself on being "the Mother of Presidents," was home to eight of the fourteen presidents pictured here. George Washington was first, of course—succeeded by men such as Madison, Jefferson, and Monroe, all of whom set a high, noble standard for America's leaders to live up to. Then came Andrew Jackson, our first Populist; Southerners like to vote for the man who says, "I'm one of you." After Jackson and the war, it would be more than a century before a man from the Deep South—Jimmy Carter—would again hold the land's highest office.

Left: Zachary Taylor of Virginia earned his nickname, "Old Rough-and-Ready," during the Mexican-American War.

Below: Another Virginia native, Woodrow Wilson, opens the 1916 American League season.

Right: President George Washington set the standard by which all successive presidents were to be judged.

Above: Whig William Henry Harrison, of the Virginia dynasty, fell ill at his inauguration and died only weeks later.

Right: An earlier Virginian president, James Monroe, drafted the Monroe Doctrine to protect the Western Hemisphere from European aggression.

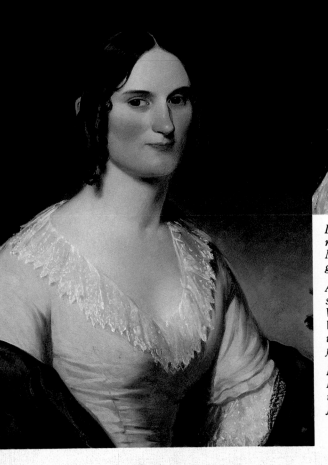

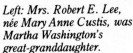

Left: Mrs. Robert E. Lee, née Mary Anne Custis, was Martha Washington's great-granddaughter.

Above: Woodrow Wilson suffered a stroke in office. Virginian Edith Bolling Galt Wilson handled matters so well that foes called her "the first lady president."

Right: Visiting England, Indian princess Pocahontas was presented at the court of James I.

Ætatis suæ 21. A°. 1616.

The old saw about the great lady standing behind every great man would hold true in the South, if it weren't for the fact that Southern women rarely stand *behind* anyone. If there's one thing Southern women have in common, it's having minds of their own. The Indian princess Pocahontas received great fame because she stood up to a man to save another man's life. Dolley Madison was one of the first of the great Washington hostesses to demonstrate that a woman could get what she wanted, and still be charming. All of these women were powerful in some way—Sarah Polk in the iron of her convictions, Rachel Jackson in her inspiration of fatal passions, Rosalynn Carter in her role as the "Steel Magnolia."

George Washington was the second husband of widow Martha Dandridge Custis (above) and stepfather to her two children. This Stuart portrait of her was never completed.

Left: Childhood sweethearts Bess and Harry Truman at their wedding in 1919.

Right: Georgian Rosalynn Smith Carter was President Jimmy Carter's full partner in politics and business.

Left: Sarah Polk of Tennessee banned wine, dancing, and card playing in the White House.

Below: Varina Howell, a wealthy Mississippi belle, married Jefferson Davis.

Right: North Carolinian Dolley Madison saved Stuart's portrait of Washington from burning.

Left: When Lyndon Johnson married Lady Bird, her wedding ring cost $2.50.

Below: Virginian Rachel Robards's divorce and subsequent marriage to Andrew Jackson caused a scandal.

Right: Ellen Arthur, also of Virginia, died before her husband, Chester, became president.

Below right: Tennessean Eliza Johnson, Andrew Johnson's first lady.

Above: Marylander John Dickinson, the "penman of the Revolution."

Below: William Ranney's painting of cavalry action at the Battle of Cowpens in South Carolina.

Left: Samuel Chase of Maryland signed the Declaration of Independence

Above: Virginia's Benjamin Harrison V, signer of the Declaration, was father and great-grandfather, respectively, of presidents William Henry Harrison and Benjamin Harrison.

Right: South Carolinian Charles Cotesworth Pinckney ran twice for the presidency as a Federalist.

The men portrayed on these pages all signed the Declaration of Independence. Above left: Charles Carroll, leader of the Revolution in Maryland. Above right: Virginian Richard Henry Lee introduced the resolution that led to the Declaration. Above: George Walton, a judge on the Supreme Court of Georgia. Below: George Read of Maryland who initially opposed the Declaration but later reluctantly signed it.

The Revolutionary South was much like the rest of the nation at the time of its birth. If you ventured far from the Eastern Seaboard, you reached the frontier. Great thought, and many of the great men, came from the cities of the coast, and Southerners such as Thomas Jefferson and John Dickinson played major roles in the conception of documents such as the Declaration of Independence and the Articles of Confederation. Southerners were always willing to fight for a cause they believed in, and seized eagerly on the crusade for independence in word and deed. Henry Lee, known as Light-Horse Harry, entered history with his eulogy for George Washington: "First in war, first in peace, and first in the hearts of his countrymen." Henry Lee's son Robert would come to inspire similar sentiment in Southerners of the next generation, fighting against the Union his father had helped create. But the hearts of the leaders of the Revolution were always with the ideal they brought into being: liberty, in the form of a nation.

In the watercolor by Jacques Le Moyne, circa 1565, Timucua Indians make offerings of native bounty at a French colony in Florida. John Mitchell's map of 1775 locates Cherokee, Choctaw, and other tribes, as thrusting state boundaries foretell the course of empire. In 1838, the Federal government exiled the Cherokee to Oklahoma. Nearly one-third of the unwilling emigrants died along the "Trail of Tears," shown at right in a painting by Robert Lindneux.

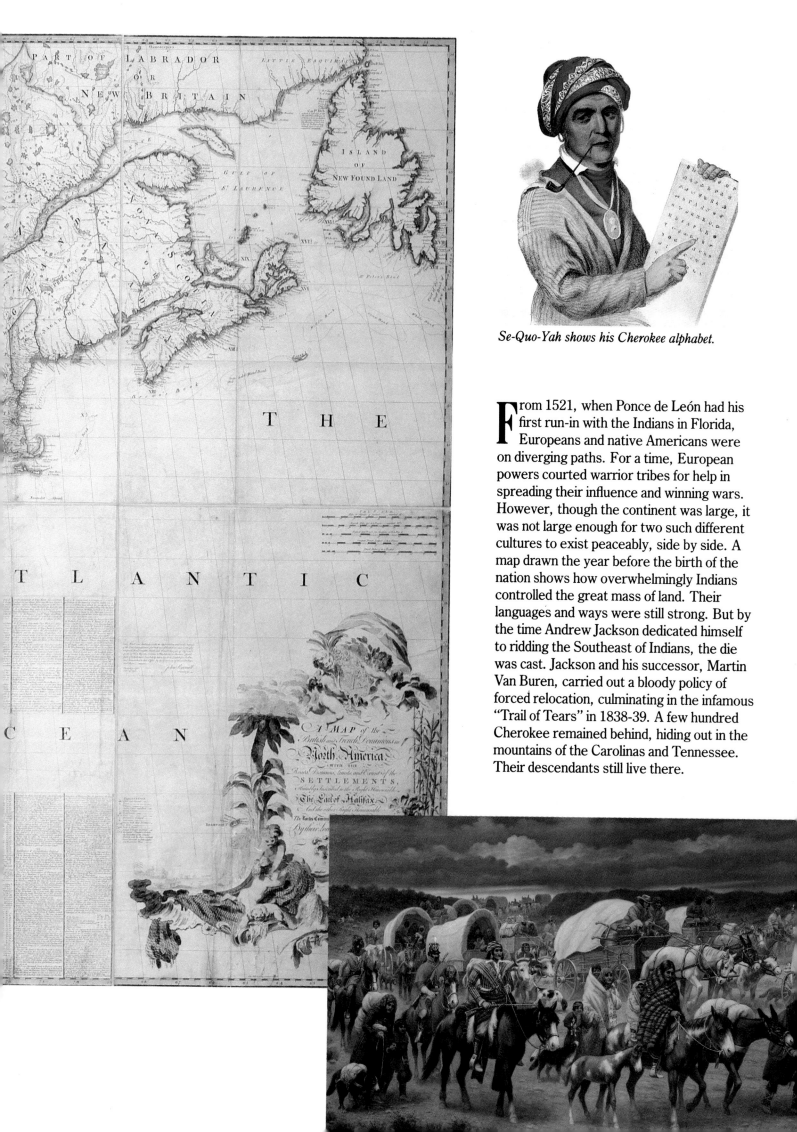

Se-Quo-Yah shows his Cherokee alphabet.

From 1521, when Ponce de León had his first run-in with the Indians in Florida, Europeans and native Americans were on diverging paths. For a time, European powers courted warrior tribes for help in spreading their influence and winning wars. However, though the continent was large, it was not large enough for two such different cultures to exist peaceably, side by side. A map drawn the year before the birth of the nation shows how overwhelmingly Indians controlled the great mass of land. Their languages and ways were still strong. But by the time Andrew Jackson dedicated himself to ridding the Southeast of Indians, the die was cast. Jackson and his successor, Martin Van Buren, carried out a bloody policy of forced relocation, culminating in the infamous "Trail of Tears" in 1838-39. A few hundred Cherokee remained behind, hiding out in the mountains of the Carolinas and Tennessee. Their descendants still live there.

A Tidewater Virginia plantation with main house and slave quarters, and a tobacco-laden ship bound for England.

Good seaports were crucial to the economic growth of the South. In the antebellum years, the most important Southern port of all was Charleston, South Carolina. The engraving at right, by W. J. Bennett, shows the Cooper River at Charleston, circa 1830.

Below: A serene view of Mount Vernon, circa 1792.

The Charleston market as painted by Charles J. Hamilton in 1872.

Was there ever a South as serene, lush, and untroubled as this? Some artists of the period were given to visual hyperbole, but it's true that the South grew, with the spread of slavery and before the onset of war, into the comfortable, genteel society revered ever since. Seaports, such as Charleston, bustled with the newfound agricultural wealth of the region. (Culture came by sailing ship, as did slaves.) The styles of life that had prevailed in the Old World were transformed into such American architectural expressions as Mount Vernon, surely one of the loveliest homes on either side of the Atlantic.

Left: The Old Plantation, *painted by an unknown artist in the late eighteenth century, depicts a celebration of African origin at a South Carolina plantation.*

Below: A View of New Orleans from the Plantation of Marigny, *rendered in 1803 by J. L. Bouqueta de Woiseri.*

Right: A symbol of westward expansion: unpretentious Independence Hall in Washington-on-the-Brazos, Texas, where the Texas Declaration of Independence from Mexico was signed on March 2, 1836.

Below right: The Moravian community of Winston-Salem, North Carolina, in 1824.

☆UNDER ☆MY☆ ☆WINGS☆ ☆ ☆EVERY☆ ☆THING

Even in the most glamorous renderings of the antebellum South, the dark edges of future calamity showed themselves. For that South was not merely "moonlight and magnolias." The grand cities and the fabulous plantations were built on the backs of slaves. And while the elegance and hospitality of Southern plantations were legendary, mixed with the legend was the romantic myth of the contented slave. Then, too, a nation growing as fast as America could not long endure two drastically different economies. There were always independent-minded Southerners, as witness the Moravians of North Carolina. And the restless expansion to the west created new controversies. Many Southerners packed up their belongings and headed out, marking their doors with the letters *G.T.T.—Gone To Texas*. But the old problems followed them to the new territories. The question of whether a state would be admitted to the Union as "slave" or "free" was one of the crucial issues that would lead to war.

Left: Robert E. Lee, then a thirty-one-year-old U.S. Army lieutenant, was urged by his wife, Mary, to have his portrait painted by William Edward West in 1838. The result so pleased Mary Lee that it was one of the few items she took with her when she moved to Richmond during the war. In contrast, the Mathew Brady photograph of Lee (taken just days after the surrender at Appomattox Courthouse on Palm Sunday in 1865) shows him as a weary, white-haired figure. Brady made the picture on the back porch of Lee's rented house in Richmond.

Robert E. Lee was the embodiment of the war, and of its contradictions. The son of a Revolutionary War hero fallen on hard times, Lee went to West Point because it guaranteed him a free education and a salaried job. He spent most of his career in far-flung Army jobs, distinguishing himself under Winfield Scott in the Mexican War. He was such a fine soldier that, when Southern states began seceding, Scott offered him command of the Union forces. Lee agonized, but finally decided he could not raise arms against his beloved Virginia. He did not approve of the war, but he never regretted his decision. After both sides got off to a faltering start, Lee emerged as the first—and perhaps the most brilliant—military genius of the war. Time and again he defeated far larger forces with his devoted troops, of whom he expected everything. The legend was born, and with it the South's first hero. Most historians recognize that, had it not been for his leadership, the war would have ended at least a year before it did. Lee left Appomattox an exhausted man—but not a defeated man. He urged swift reconciliation, and he never stopped trying to build a new South from the ashes of war.

46

Above left: Lieutenant General Stephen Lee.

Center left: Lieutenant General Jubal Early.

Left: Major General Richard Ewell.

Above: Major General Nathan Forrest.

Right: Major General George Pickett.

Below: Lieutenant General James ("Old Pete") Longstreet.

The men Lee gathered around him made up an extraordinary cross section of the South's brightest and best. So capable were Lee's lieutenants that Abraham Lincoln was heard to complain that the good generals were all fighting for the other side. Lee knew each of these men in the most subtle fashion. He went out of his way to stay out of squabbles among them, to use the peculiarities and strengths of each to the fullest advantage in a tactical plan, to play them against each other. But when a battle went badly, "the Old Man" took the blame.

Far left: Lieutenant General Wade Hampton opposed secession but served in the Army of the Confederacy.

Left: Five wounds at Sharpsburg failed to deter Brigadier General John Gordon.

Below: Lieutenant General John Hood unsuccessfully opposed, at Atlanta, Sherman's march to the sea.

Left: Ironically, General Thomas ("Stonewall") Jackson died after being wounded, in the confusion of battle, by his own men.

Above: West Point graduate Major General Daniel Hill was a mathematics professor at the time he joined the Confederate army.

Below: Brigadier General Braxton Bragg suffered defeat at Shiloh.

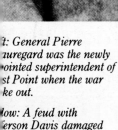

t: General Pierre uregard was the newly ointed superintendent of st Point when the war ke out.

low: A feud with erson Davis damaged neral Joseph Johnston's litary career.

Left: Lieutenant General Ambrose Hill was highly considered by Lee.

Above Hill: Colonel John Mosby scouted for Stuart and later formed his own group of irregulars, Mosby's Rangers.

Right: Brigadier General J. E. B. Stuart died from the wounds he received at Yellow Tavern.

"My fraternity brothers at Chapel Hill once took me to the secret room where they kept records of everyone who'd ever been a member. They write a line or two about what happened to you in your life, and when you died. There were seven boys in the class of 1863—and six of them were dead two years later. Those boys were going to be the leaders of North Carolina. They were the college generation, and that generation was just decimated. Decimated, though, isn't the word, because that just means one in ten." The two pages following show Confederate veterans gathered for a reunion at Louisville in 1905.

Left: Cotton-Picking Time, *a not-so-primitive painting by "Aunt" Clara McDonald Williamson of Iredell, Texas (circa 1953). Above: Bonneted against the sun, a North Carolina farm woman leans on her hoe (1940).*

The world had never seen a better place to grow cotton than the antebellum South—the climate was right, the soil was rich, and the immense amount of labor needed to cultivate it was available cheaply—and ruinously—through the system of slavery. Fortunes were made quickly. So great were the needs of the textile mills of the North and of Great Britain that the South, by the mid-nineteenth century, managed to convince itself that cotton was "King." Secessionists urged the South toward war, on the commonly held and near-religious notion that Britain would have to side with the supplier of its most important raw material. South Carolina senator James Hammond put it this way to the Senate in 1858: "Without firing a gun, without drawing a sword, should they make war on us we would bring the whole world to our feet. . . . What would happen if no cotton was furnished for three years? This is certain: England would topple headlong and carry the whole civilized world with her, save the South. No, you dare not make war on cotton. No power on earth dares to make war upon it, Cotton *is* King." But this proclamation helped lead the South to disaster. The North blockaded cotton ports, blockade-runners were able to bring only a little of the South's cotton to the world, Britain stayed neutral, and the South, deprived of its chief income, was brought to its knees.

Loaded to nerve-racking capacity, the stern-wheeler Katie Robbins *is bound for Vicksburg, Mississippi. The cotton and the photo are both vintage 1884.*

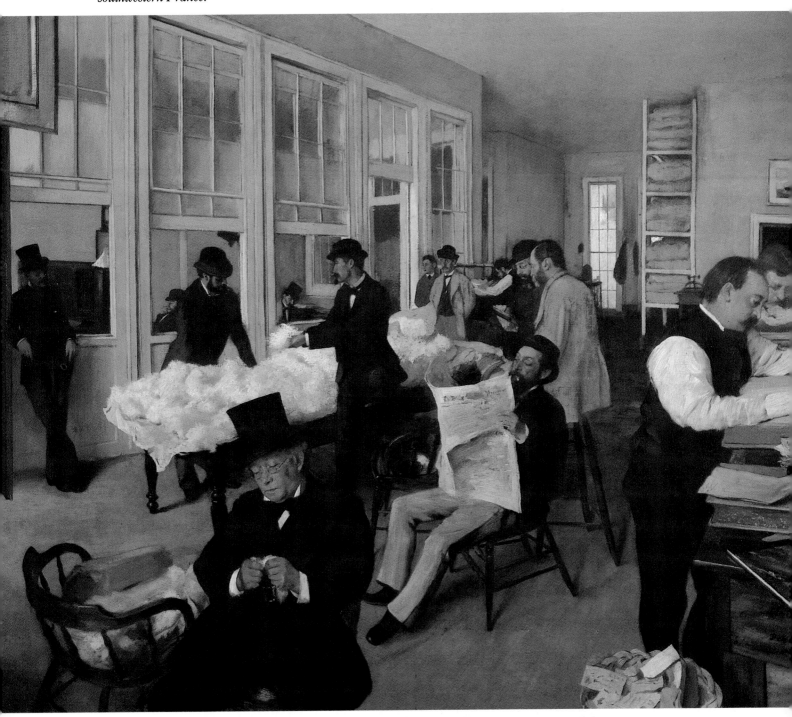

French Impressionist Edgar Degas painted the proceedings at his relatives' cotton brokerage during a visit to New Orleans in 1873. The original painting now hangs in the Musée des Beaux-Arts at Pau, in southwestern France.

Frontier states such as Alabama and Mississippi became surprisingly rich while cotton was king; before the war, Mississippi had more millionaires per capita than any other state in the Union. A planter would load his crop on wagons or riverboats, head for the cotton exchange downriver (New Orleans, Memphis, Mobile, and Charleston were among the most active), and watch the efforts of his slaves converted to gold. After the war, the labor necessary to bring in a good crop was no longer available free, and there were several disasters in the price of cotton. Land was exhausted by overfarming of this nutrient-thirsty crop. Attacks by waves of boll weevils put many planters out of business forever, but taught others to rotate their crops and try planting other things. The grateful town of Enterprise, Alabama, even raised a monument to the lowly insect for teaching this lesson.

The critical chores of tobacco farming were done together. The neighbors would come and help you string your tobacco, and hang it in the barn for curing, then you would go down the road and help them with theirs. I was a hander. I'd take five or six leaves, I forget, and hand to an experienced stringer, who would take them, make a twist with the tobacco twine around the stick, then with his other hand reach for another handful of tobacco, so that he would end up with the tobacco hanging neatly from both sides of the stick. Then that would hang in the barn for curing. My grandmother used to tell me about market day. The auctioneer would stop at your pile of tobacco, and there would follow a ten- or fifteen-second auction. He would pay in cash. And that would be all the money the family would see that year.

Left: The Rigsbees, father and son, sow tobacco plants in Chatham County, North Carolina, in 1940.

Right: A Lumberton, North Carolina, tobacco market auction, 1976.

Below: Workers string leaves for drying on a tobacco farm near Maxton, North Carolina, in 1959.

Signs leave no doubt that it is Mr. Betancourt and Mr. Culmer rolling cigars in Tampa. Mr. Culmer obviously enjoys his product (circa 1970).

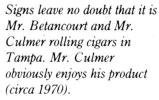

Above: Virginians May and Lily tend to their hens, circa 1890.

Left: Women of the Raymond, Georgia, community council grade and pack the cooperative's first cases of eggs (1921).

Overleaf: Some three dozen apple pickers pause for a portrait in Berkeley County, West Virginia (1910). The stencil tells us that the apples are York Imperials.

Above: Handsomely accoutred, Berkeley Adams of Red Oak, Virginia, cradles his prize-winning ears of corn (1909).

Left: Young Joe Eggleston, Jr., stands tall on his own acre of Virginia corn (1917).

Overleaf: A thriving field of pumpkin and squash in North Carolina (circa 1927).

The TEN TON COW!

This cow gave over 20,000 lbs. (2,353 gallons) of milk and 745 lbs. of butter during last 10 months. Owned by Peabody College, Nashville, Tenn.

If you've ever spent time on a farm in the South you likely know what it's like to arise before the sun, stumble out into the cool darkness, make your way to the barn, and begin the very first chore of the day—the milking. And chances are you remember the magnificence of warm, fresh milk, with all its butterfat. As towns grew and people turned to specialized forms of farming, the dairy increased in importance. The milkman's wagon became a familiar, welcome sight—always in the cool of the day. Some cows, like the Tennessee record holder at left, became justly renowned for their productivity.

Below left: A well-tended cow at the demonstration farm at Peabody College, Tennessee (circa 1930). Left: The Cliff Owen dairy farm in Winchester, Kentucky (circa 1905). Above: A motorcycle with sidecar speeds the product from the Ewing Dairy in Louisville (1928). Below: Dairyman Charles Scharer of Roane County, Tennessee, surveys his handsome herd.

And they cleave it
And cleave it. Loins. Ham.
    Shoulder. Feet. Chops.

Even the tail's an obscure prize.
Goes into buckets; the child hauls

From hand to hand the pail all dripping.
Top of the heap, tremulous as water, lies
The big maroon liver.

    And the women receive it.
Gravely waiting as for supper grace.

        —Fred Chappell, "February"

Above: The Farm of Theodor Frick, Porkpacker, at Brook Avenue, *painted by Carl Hambuck of Richmond in 1878. Left: Hog butchering in New Marker, Maryland. Below: County agent weighs a pig in Craven County, North Carolina (1929).*

ogs aren't the only livestock Southerners prize. Above, a turn-of-the-century Wilcox County, Alabama, woman displays a fine turkey; below, Mrs. A. D. McDonald of San Antonio holds her prize-winning cockerel, 1931. At right are members of the 1930 Oklahoma A&M College livestock judging team. These proud gentlemen won first place in that year's International Livestock Show in Chicago.

Overleaf: Livestock show and rodeo at Houston's Astrodome, 1972.

Showing their stuff, proud farmers pose with crops and livestock. Newton ("Watermelon") Cooper of Vicksburg, Mississippi (above left, circa 1910), grew a 50-pound specimen. Amanda Vicknair, the "Squash Lady" of Killona, Louisiana, shows off a prize gourd (right, 1969). Crops can also have broad economic impact. At left, seed company president Robert R. Coker of Hartsville, South Carolina, studies a variety of wheat developed to revolutionize the state's agricultural industry. Less innovative, but perhaps more delicious, is the succulent Houston fig crop, top right, circa 1910.

When you are a very small child, an honest-to-goodness roller coaster seems the largest and most wonderful contraption on earth. Even when you grow up, a fair is a marvelous place to be. In the South of yesterday, a trip to the county or state fair was often the only vacation a family took. You could display the fruits of your labors, and even buy a reward in the form of a kiss. (The sign below makes me wonder just who E. A. Ramsey might have been.)

Left: A fancywork booth at the Eastern Star Lawn Carnival in Cumberland, Maryland, circa 1910. At right, members of the Boy's Pig Club of Auburn, Alabama, call for attention (1919). Below: Luna Park in downtown Houston (1915). Below left: Five-cent kisses for sale at the Tri-State Fair, Memphis, circa 1920.

We all love holidays. Fourth of July is an ideal time for a family get-together. The group at left is savoring fried fish on the Cane River near Natchitoches, Louisiana, 1940. Lillie and Mary Kenney of San Antonio (below, circa 1910) look appropriately cherubic on Valentine's Day. The face of the Natchez, Mississippi, youngster pictured above (circa 1895) reflects the excitement and anticipation of Christmas.

Left: Mary Irvin, the "Most Beautiful Baby" in Wharton County, Texas.

Below: The circus comes to Hendersonville, North Carolina.

Right: Washington, D.C.'s Bury's Drugstore drapes itself in Old Glory for the Fourth of July. All photos are from the early 1900s.

The South, in the early part of this century, could be a lonely place. It was such a rural society that a holiday celebration became a very important thing—a social event, an excuse for people to get together. People who rarely took a day off from the fields would put on their finery, head into town, and spend a day in the midst of a homegrown spectacle. On Memorial Day, veterans of the Civil War (and later conflicts) would squeeze into their old uniforms, gather behind their old colors, and parade proudly through the town square. When the circus came to Hendersonville, North Carolina, bearing elaborate signs announcing all manner of amusements—"10 Big Shows!"—people gathered on every available inch of sidewalk. Kids would take turns chasing the exotic animals along the parade route, and out to the circus tents on the edge of town. Imagine how strange the first glimpse of a camel must have been for a farm boy who'd never seen anything odder than a Jersey milk cow.

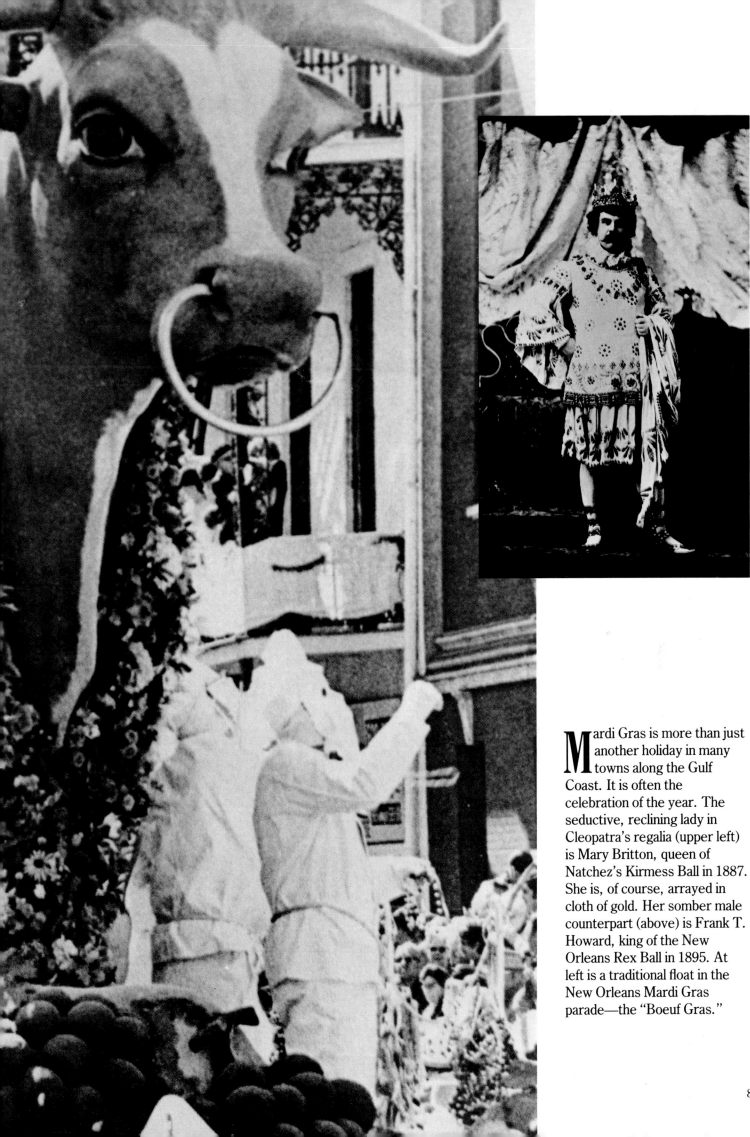

Mardi Gras is more than just another holiday in many towns along the Gulf Coast. It is often the celebration of the year. The seductive, reclining lady in Cleopatra's regalia (upper left) is Mary Britton, queen of Natchez's Kirmess Ball in 1887. She is, of course, arrayed in cloth of gold. Her somber male counterpart (above) is Frank T. Howard, king of the New Orleans Rex Ball in 1895. At left is a traditional float in the New Orleans Mardi Gras parade—the "Boeuf Gras."

No child can resist dressing up—be it in a spunky Felix the Cat costume like the one worn by ten-year-old Texan Portia Porter (lower right corner, circa 1926) or as one of a dignified constellation of Christmas stars at Louisville's Christian Church Orphan's Home (below right, circa 1926). Any holiday can be an excuse for dressing up: the boys from the Cathedral School in Natchez donned their sailor suits for Columbus Day, 1895 (lower extreme left). Miss Ernestine Edmunds of St. Hedwig School in Texas had her students dress up as American Indians in honor of Thanksgiving, 1918 (right). The mixed bag of outfits in the picture in the upper right corner was assembled in commemoration of the 1940 Memphis Cotton Carnival.

The children in the
mock-marriage taking place in
1963 at Charlotte, North
Carolina (above), find it hard
to take marriage seriously.
Well-wishers bid bon voyage to
Dr. and Mrs. Victor Miller
(right) as they leave for their
honeymoon from the train
station in Hagerstown,
Maryland, 1905.

Overleaf: In Atlanta, a very
serious bridal party anticipates
the wedding of John Schaffner
Spalding and Mary
Temperance Connally in 1902.

W eddings are the beginning of a family
album. Children complete the
picture. The four generations of
Louisville women (left, circa 1920)
represent an enviable unbroken family
line. Above, a proud father, Dean
Crawford of Louisville, and his shy son,
photographed about 1940, represent the
male branch of a family tree. The complex
bonds between family members
have long fascinated Southern writers.

Children, who all look pretty much alike on the day they are born, swiftly adopt roles and poses that reflect their places in society. The pair of Cajun girls above and the little Natchez dandies below are not far apart in age or geography, but whole worlds already separate them. When the parents were poor, a visit to the portrait photographer was an exercise in hopeful projection—the kids were made to look as shiny and bright as their parents' best hopes for them. The finest attire came out of the cedar chest (or was stitched up for the occasion). Hair was washed, combed, brushed, and either curled or slicked down. Faces and feet were scrubbed. Maybe all the soap and water explains the solemn expressions on these children's faces.

The gift of growing up gracefully is handed out unevenly. Here are recorded stops along the way to maturity for eight Southern youngsters. They range from the children of early nineteenth century Baltimore gentry (complete with retriever) to two young ladies photographed in the 1940s in Heber Springs, Arkansas, doing quite well, thank you, in what may well be their first long dresses. In retrospect, these mementos return us to the pains, pleasures, trials, and triumphs of the passage from childhood to adolescence.

Bespectacled, closely cropped, but dressed in lace, Margaret Wood was photographed in Victoria, Texas (circa 1910).
Left: The Westwood children, painted by black portrait artist Joshua Johnson of Baltimore (circa 1807).
Below, opposite page: San Antonio's Patricia Young reluctantly shares her picture book (circa 1926).

Left: A serene rendering of Clara Mazureau, the daughter of a successful New Orleans barrister, painted by Jacques Amans in 1838.
Above: Sisters Picola and Iola Harper of Heber Springs, Arkansas, exhibit a nervous dignity in elegant, long ball gowns (1940s).

Left: A grinning Georgia family relishes some splendid summer watermelon (circa 1910), while the John Minor Botts family of Virginia strikes a more reserved pose in what was probably a more difficult time (circa 1865).

Overleaf: All present and accounted for. The Thompson family gets together in Tattnall County, Georgia, around the turn of the century.

Left: A baptism in South Carolina, 1929-30.
Below: Church women in Person County, North Carolina, pause during "cleanup" day in 1939.
Right: The interior of an Alabama church, 1939.

People went great distances to get to church, and I don't believe it had so much to do with religious fervor as with a chance to see people. Sometimes, on Sunday in the South, I see people coming out of church, and they stand around outside for an hour, even if there's no dinner-on-the-grounds. When church is over up North, people go home. In the old days, they would walk to wherever there was a preaching. It wasn't until the circuit-riding Baptist and Methodist ministers came along that churches sprang up in the countryside. There's no event so joyous as a church supper or a dinner-on-the-grounds, because it really is a bringing-together of the whole community. Mattie Lou O'Kelley's remembered vision shows how much life happens at such an event.

Overleaf: Mattie Lou O'Kelley's happy memories of growing up in Maysville, Georgia, include All-Day Dinner on the Grounds of the Grove Level Baptist Church.

103

We were surely the most poorly educated of all the regions. Many Southerners of earlier generations couldn't afford to send their children all the way through grade school, so that college to these people was a distant, unimaginable dream. But just because we didn't have many schools didn't mean that we didn't respect an education. On the contrary. I suspect that education was highly prized in the South because parents saw how useful an education would have been to them. Education took on an importance far beyond the normal proportions. I know of many families where the mother and father were both uneducated, but were willing to sacrifice anything to send their children to school. Often the skills learned were aimed at a specific job, but time spent socializing was valuable, too.

Opposite page: A very early campus photograph taken at Salem Academy and College in North Carolina, 1858. Top left: Students in the Capitol's Statuary Hall, circa 1898. Top right: Printer's-devils-to-be, Shawnee High School, Louisville, 1939. Above left: Chafing-dish cookery in a dorm at Brenau College, Georgia, 1912. Above right: A class in cheese making at Hampton Institute, Virginia, circa 1899. At left: A busload in Bullitt County, Kentucky, circa 1930.

A Jefferson County Free Library bookmobile stops at the Sayre commissary station in the western part of the county in the 1920s. Many years later, in 1970, the Hicks children and a visiting relative wait for a morning bus to take them to school in Avery County, North Carolina. School starts in mid-August to allow for "snow days," during which buses will not be able to drive over hazardous icy mountain roads. Education in the rural South has been a matter that turned, variously, on attitudes, distances, finances—and wheels.

Left: Juliette Low founded the Girl Scouts in Savannah in 1912. Here she awards a Golden Eaglet, the GSA's highest achievement.

Below: William R. Davie (1800), principal founder and trustee of the University of North Carolina.

Right: Booker T. Washington of Virginia, the former slave who founded Tuskegee Institute (1881).

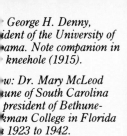

George H. Denny,
ident of the University of
ama. Note companion in
kneehole (1915).

w: Dr. Mary McLeod
une of South Carolina
president of Bethune-
man College in Florida
1923 to 1942.

t: Martha Berry of
gia founded Berry College
6) which emphasized
tional skills.

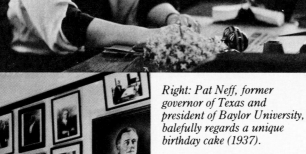

Right: Pat Neff, former
governor of Texas and
president of Baylor University,
balefully regards a unique
birthday cake (1937).

Below: Blind, deaf Helen
Keller of Alabama overcame
handicaps to graduate from
Radcliffe in 1904.

Bottom: New Orleans educator
and welfare worker Sophie Bell
Wright, portrayed circa 1904.

Above: Teacher of physical
education at U.T.-Austin in
the 1920s, Eunice Aden sports
the requisite middy blouse and
bloomers.

Below: George Washington
Carver, named a Royal Fellow
in 1916, conducted his
brilliant research with peanuts
while teaching at Tuskegee
Institute (circa 1930).

Their faces may not be familiar, but their
names ring out. These are a few of the
Southerners who helped lift our region
from its intellectual poverty, and their
names appear on campus buildings all over
the South. Booker T. Washington went to
Tuskegee and convinced the black farmers
there to help build a school. The students
built the school (the first course was
bricklaying), and the rest is history. George
Washington Carver went there and began
the peanut revolution—he developed more
than three hundred products that could be
made from what had been regarded as a
lowly crop. To this day Tuskegee has the
feeling of a school that was built by hungry
minds. Helen Keller's unconquerable spirit
became a beacon of hope to the entire
world, and of course, Juliette Low is
responsible for generations of civic-minded
women.

Right: Johns Hopkins School of Medicine, circa 1890.

Left: Dr. Anita Newcomb McGee of Washington, D.C. built a corps of Army nurses, late 1800s.

Below: A Red Cross dental clinic in Kentucky, circa 1932.

Left: Drs. J. W. Allen and D. Emory Allen of Content, Texas, 1905.

Right and far right: Houston's finest: heart specialists Dr. Denton Cooley, surgeon-in-chief at Texas Heart Institute, and Dr. Michael De Bakey, chancellor of Baylor College of Medicine.

eft: Dr. Gaine annon, Appalachia.

elow: Houston urses, circa 1925.

ight: Dr. Samuel 'udd, exiled for tting John Wilkes ooth's broken leg.

ar right: Virginia's alter Reed isolated osquito responsible r yellow fever.

Everyone has fond, romantic memories of the Southern country doctor making his house calls—everyone, that is, except the country doctor. He remembers a time when, in the lives of many rural people, the doctor's bag was the only source of health care. His hours were long, and he could never do enough. The Civil War forced great strides in medicine, particularly the use of anesthetics and sanitary standards. But epidemics were more fearful than wars; the South was a harrowing battleground for yellow fever even after Walter Reed identified its source. Today the South is home to some of the most advanced schools of medicine in the world—witness the renowned centers in Houston and Birmingham.

Left: In his stories, George Washington Cable of New Orleans showed uncommon sensitivity to the plight of blacks.

Right: St. Louis-born Kate Chopin wrote about New Orleans with the insight of a native.

Below: After the death of his young wife, a nightmare world closed in on Richmond's Edgar Allan Poe.

Above: Author of To Kill a Mockingbird, Harper Lee seems glad to be back in her hometown of Monroeville, Alabama (1962).

Above right: Texan Katherine Anne Porter had been an actress and a reporter before winning the Pulitzer Prize for a volume of her collected stories.

Right: James Agee drew from his rural Tennessee roots in Let Us Now Praise Famous Men, published in 1941.

Left: North Carolinian William Sydney Porter, better known as O. Henry, was famous for the ironic twists to his short stories (circa 1900).

Above: Oklahoman Ralph Ellison's Invisible Man won the 1953 National Book Award.

Right: The genteel Virginia upbringing of Ellen Glasgow shaped her incisive, socially conscious novels. She won the Pulitzer Prize in 1942.

Above: A former Pinkerton private eye, Dashiell Hammett of Baltimore used his experience as background for his detective novels.

Right: William Faulkner, the 1949 Nobel Prize laureate, wrote in a style that merged poetry with stream of consciousness in novels such as The Sound and the Fury and As I Lay Dying.

Left: Atlanta-born James Dickey is a novelist and poet-in-residence at the University of South Carolina.

Right: Born in Joplin, Missouri, poet and playwright Langston Hughes was an important member of the Harlem Renaissance.

Below: Eudora Welty of Mississippi is a storyteller known for the evocative charm of her short fiction.

Perhaps, as Eudora Welty has jokingly remarked, there's something in the water down here. More likely, it has to do with our dozens of dialects, our love of talking, of stories, of those who tell them. Surely no region in the world has been recorded in words as obsessively as the South—or as well. The Southern writer had among his or her materials passion and hardship, greatness and meanness, love and its opposite. Most of all the South has known struggle, and it is from struggle that the great books are born. Sometimes the consciousness at work is epic: William Faulkner's vast vision of Yoknapatawpha County, Mark Twain's pair of indomitable classics, Thomas Wolfe's enormous novelistic slices of memory, Robert Penn Warren's unforgettable *All the King's Men*. With other writers, it is the clarity of a specific place and variety of people that we admire: Miss Welty's jewel-like tales, the misfits of Flannery O'Connor, the elegant sadness of Truman Capote's odd world. These writers have created our myth.

Left: Alabama's Walker Percy (shown here with his grandson) left the medical profession and pursued his interest in writing after a serious bout with tuberculosis.

Below: Author of the brilliant novel All the King's Men, *Robert Penn Warren of Kentucky was recently named America's poet laureate.*

Above: Virginian Douglas Southall Freeman in his digs. Freeman's monumental R. E. Lee *(four volumes) won the Pulitzer Prize in 1935.*

Right: In the 1920s, Zora Neale Hurston left Florida for New York City to become a major figure in the Harlem Renaissance movement.

Left: A childhood neighbor of Harper Lee, Truman Capote gave his own account of growing up in the South in The Grass Harp.

Above: Savannah-born Flannery O'Connor wove Catholic mysticism into her vivid novels and short stories.

Right: The daughter of missionary parents, West Virginian Pearl Buck drew on her experiences in China to write The Good Earth.

ve: Richard Wright's
biographical Black Boy
ng from memories of
Mississippi boyhood.

t: Georgian Joel
ndler Harris delighted
dren with his Uncle
us tales (circa 1905).

w: Missouri's Samuel
mens, under the pen
e of Mark Twain,
e the American classics
1 Sawyer and
kleberry Finn.

Right: Thomas Wolfe based
Look Homeward, Angel *on*
his childhood spent at his
mother's boardinghouse in
Asheville, North Carolina
(circa 1938).

Below: In 1967, Virginian
William Styron sparked great
controversy with his searing
account of an 1831 slave
uprising in The Confessions
of Nat Turner.

Many a Southerner is born with a flair for drama. For the flamboyant Tallulah Bankhead, the world was the audience, and acting only one emotional outlet. Her celebrity eventually grew to match her outsized personality. Some of this nation's great playwrights have also come from the South. The plays of Tennessee Williams are complex, intuitive studies of Southern life. Lillian Hellman ranks high as both an essayist and a playwright. By mingling their lives with their art, Southerners have given insight into the unique aspects of the Southern experience.

Above left: Maryland's Edwin Booth as Hamlet (circa 1878).

Above: Cat on a Hot Tin Roof, *a steamy reflection life in the South, won Tennessee Williams a Pulitzer Prize in 1955.*

Below: Charleston's DuBose Heyward wrote t novel Porgy *in 1925, upo which was based the class musical* Porgy and Bess. *(A scene from the 1936 production is shown at le*

Left: Speakeasy queen Texas Guinan reputedly did not drink the gin she sold.

Below: Alabama's Tallulah Bankhead as Regina Giddens in The Little Foxes *(1939).*

Right: Ethel Waters offers a shoulder to Georgian Carson McCullers at the opening night party for Member of the Wedding *in 1950. The "youngster" at the right is the star, Julie Harris.*

Left: Unafraid of offbeat roles, Rip Torn satirized the eccentricities of fellow Texan Howard Hughes in Sam Shepard's play Seduced.

Right: Lillian Hellman wove her personal view of fellow Southerners into The Little Foxes.

Far right: Erskine Caldwell, whose Tobacco Road *enjoyed a record Broadway run.*

Above: Tom Mix was a U.S. marshal before he was a Hollywood cowboy star. Left: Texan Ann Sheridan was tagged the "Oomph Girl" (1938). Below: Her portrayal of Loretta Lynn in Coal Miner's Daughter won Sissy Spacek an Oscar.

Above: Joanne Woodward in No Down Payment (1957). Above right: Dorothy Lamour, a former Miss New Orleans, with Bing Crosby and Bob Hope. Below: Kentuckian D. W. Griffith (right) with Douglas Fairbanks, Sr., Mary Pickford, and Charles Chaplin (1919).

Above: In this scene from Gone with the Wind, Scarlett O'Hara and Ashley Wilkes rendezvous at Twelve Oaks. Right: Savannah-born Miriam Hopkins played the Southern belle in many films of the thirties.

Above: A lovelorn soldier gazes at Lillian Gish in the 1915 masterpiece The Birth of a Nation. Left: Georgian Charles Coburn, a Hollywood character actor. Right: Florida-born Faye Dunaway.

Films made by Southerners about the South differ from those done by outsiders. D. W. Griffith's stirring *The Birth of a Nation* reflected, in good part, his father's experience as a Confederate soldier. Tennessee Williams was equally subjective in probing the psyche of a Southern belle in *A Streetcar Named Desire.* The classic representation of the South, MGM's romantic *Gone with the Wind,* was cast, ironically, with two English actors in starring roles and was scored by Viennese Max Steiner. A bit more accurate portrayal was *Showboat,* touched with a sensibility part Mark Twain, part Hollywood and Vine. At least Irene Dunne, cast as the heroine, was from Kentucky. Other individual Southern contributions to the golden age of cinema were delightful: straight-shooting Tom Mix and Gene Autry; glamorous Mae Murray, Ann Sheridan, Dorothy Lamour, and Ava Gardner; antic Oliver Hardy; and versatile Charles Coburn.

Below: Georgian Burt Reynolds. Right: Texan Mary Martin in Kiss the Boys Goodbye *(1941). Far right: Tony Curtis and Miami-born Sidney Poitier in* The Defiant Ones *(1958).*

Above: Virginian Bill ("Bojangles") Robinson with Shirley Temple in The Little Colonel *(1935). Left: Joseph Cotten hailed from Richmond, Virginia. Right: Ava Gardner came from a tiny farm town in North Carolina.*

...ft: Atlantan Oliver ...ardy. Right: ...uisville's Irene ...unne in the 1936 ...rsion of Showboat. *...elow: Arkansas ...ooner Dick Powell.*

Above: Former Ziegfeld girl Mae Murray, circa 1925. Above Murray: Blanche Dubois (Vivien Leigh) waits for A Streetcar Named Desire *in the 1951 film version of Tennessee Williams's play. Right: Gene Autry, the "Singing Cowboy."*

44-15

Below: Margaret Mitchell was an Atlanta newspaper journalist before she wrote Gone with the Wind. *Here she interviews Georgia Tech students in 1922.*

Right: Carl Murphy was publisher of Baltimore's Afro-American Newspapers, 1918-44.

Above: The staff of Progressive Farmer *in the 1920s: P. T. Hines, J. L. Mayford, G. H. Alford, Clarence Poe, John Pearson, and Tait Butler.*

Left: Hodding Carter III, editor of the Delta Democrat-Times *(Greenville, Mississippi) until 1977.*

Below: North Carolinian Edward R. Murrow broadcast from London during the blitz in WW II.

Left: CBS anchorman Dan Rather attended law school in Texas before turning journalist.

Below: Josephus Daniels, editor of Raleigh's News and Observer, *served as secretary of the navy from 1913 to 1921. FDR is to be glimpsed behind naval officer.*

Right: Mississippi's Red Barber was the popular announcer for the Brooklyn Dodgers in the 1940s.

As a young man, I was in love with the writings of H. L. Mencken. Though his famous essay describing the South as "The Sahara of the Bozart" had a certain ring of truth, our region has produced many of the best in Mencken's own field. The Carters of Mississippi are now in their third generation as newspaper publishers. Red Barber became the broadcast "Verce of the Brooklyn Dodgers." Nationally syndicated sportswriter Grantland Rice could never resist a rhyme. Ralph McGill and his *Atlanta Constitution* were outspoken voices of liberalism in a time when that was a dangerous stance. Miriam Leslie was so involved in the fight to save her husband's publishing empire that she changed her name to Frank Leslie after he died. And many of today's top television newspeople got their start down here, including my colleagues Dan Rather and Diane Sawyer.

Left: Baltimore's H. L. Mencken used caustic wit to skewer the less sophisticated.

Top right: Columnist Dorothy Dix (born Elizabeth Gilmer, in Tennessee) was the world's highest-paid woman writer in the 1920s.

Center right: Tennessee sportswriter Grantland Rice could not resist a clever rhyme.

Right: Oklahoman Bill Moyers.

Left: Ralph McGill at the controls of the Atlanta Constitution.

Far above: Tarheel David Brinkley.

Above: New Orleans-born Miriam Leslie restored husband Frank's failing publishing empire.

Below: Diane Sawyer of Kentucky.

Southerners love to express themselves with emphasis, and some of our most emphatic expressions are through music. (What could be more emphatic than the young Elvis Presley stomping through "Blue Suede Shoes"?) And then there's the sweet, sad sound of a mountain fiddler and somebody singing the old standard ballads. But even in the slickest, most electrified Nashville songs of today, you can hear the origins of Southern music—which includes most forms of American music. Jazz, blues, gospel, bluegrass, Sacred Harp, country, and even rock 'n' roll got their start in the South. Maybe it's because we've been poor. It's hard times that give rise to folk music. All the old English and Scottish ballads are about some tragedy worth remembering—a boy who died for love, a woman who gave her life for her man. All these rich veins of music pulsed amid poverty and trouble. Look at Loretta Lynn, Dolly Parton, Hank Williams, Willie Nelson, Johnny Cash, Louis Armstrong, Mahalia Jackson. These people came from hard times, and their art was created from what they remembered. Perhaps that's what made them play.

Left: Hank Williams's poignant vocal style assured him a spot in the Country Music Hall of Fame.

Above: His trumpet was his trademark: Louis ("Satchmo") Armstrong debuted outside New Orleans with King Oliver's band.

Right: New Orleans-born composer Louis Gottschalk gave his first piano concert at age eight.

Above: Bandleader Kay Kyser, a North Carolinian, teamed up with vivacious Texan Ann Miller in the 1944 film Jam Session.

Right: A 1949 photograph of Billie ("Lady Day") Holiday, ten years before her death.

Below: Kentuckian "Stringbean" David Akeman's down-home blend of banjo picking and humor was popular with Grand Ole Opry audiences.

Right: "Sweet Dreams," one of Patsy Cline's greatest hits, was released just weeks after her tragic death in 1963.

Below: The Everly Brothers' use of close harmony in songs like "Devoted to You" influenced Bob Dylan and the Beatles.

Left: To protect the morals of impressionable teenage America, Elvis Presley was shown only from the waist up on "The Ed Sullivan Show."

Above: Legendary blues singer Bessie Smith was a native of Chattanooga.

Right: Schoolgirl Dolly Parton had the infectious grin of the famous singer she was to become.

Above: After college in Alabama, W. C. Handy formed his own band in 1903. He composed "St. Louis Blues" in 1914.

Right: Mahalia Jackson's stirring gospel singing was heard at Carnegie Hall and at John F. Kennedy's inauguration.

Above: Johnny Cash, a sharecropper's son, began writing songs at age twelve.

Right: Janis Joplin epitomized the hard edge of rock 'n' roll in the sixties.

Below: Loretta Lynn and Conway Twitty won a collaborative Grammy in 1971.

Above: Nat ("King") Cole was the first black artist to have his own television variety series.

Right: The Original Carter Family were country music pioneers. A. P. and his wife, Sara, stand behind his sister-in-law Maybelle, whose daughter June is married to Johnny Cash (circa 1928).

Below: The Drum and Bugle Corps of Louisville's St. Peter Claver School (1941).

Left: Texan Van Cliburn was the first American to win Moscow's International Tchaikovsky Piano Competition.

Above: New Orleans trumpeter "Kid Punch" Miller heads to or from a gig.

Right: Country music's Willie Nelson also has the versatility to do standards like "Blue Skies" and "Star Dust."

The first and probably, at the time, the only band in Gatesville, Texas, 1875.

TWO

History is important to you as a Southerner mainly if it's something that happened to your Uncle Bob. As I've said, a society as rural as the South was, in the early days of our nation, simply didn't have the means, the time, or the inclination to follow events as they happened. But as a region we've had our fair share of big events, and, as they always do, these events produced great heroes—and a few notable villains.

At the time he was elected, surely, Andrew Jackson was the greatest hero to come out of the South. Today the word "revolutionary" is tossed around too much; every new gadget is revolutionary. But Jackson's presidency was as close to being genuinely revolutionary as any we have had. His was the first truly popular election. He was elected by the people, and his election was looked upon as the triumph of the people over the narrow group of aristocrats who had run things heretofore.

I'm thinking particularly of the famous story of his inauguration, when seemingly half of his rough-hewn frontier constituency showed up at the White House, and proceeded to wreck the place. Proper people—which at the time meant mostly Yankees—were mortified at the idea of all the muddy boots on velvet, the hillbillies in the temple. (Their indignation was, in some sense, echoed by the guffaws and cartoons that ensued when Jimmy Carter took office in 1976.)

When Jackson came to power and the rabble came to the capital, many educated people thought the American experiment with liberty was over. They supposed that the day of mob rule was finally upon them; and, in fact, this came uncomfortably close to the truth. There *was* a streak of demagogue in Jackson, and when he challenged the Supreme Court he really meant it: "To hell with you guys in robes. I'm the President now."

I have at home a painting, a portrait of Jackson from the time, by some anonymous admirer of his. It shows him in formal dress with his hand on the map of the American empire, standing beside an arch. It was uncharacteristic of Jackson, but it was the way many Southerners thought of him—as a kind of demigod, a Southern Caesar.

He was a firebrand. He was ready to kill anybody, anytime, for any reason. We North Carolinians like to say he was born in North Carolina—South Carolinians say South Carolina. At any rate, he was born in the community of Waxhaw, which was right on the state line. As people did in those days, he

Thomas Sully's portrait of General Andrew Jackson, painted in 1819, from which a popular engraving was made.

read for the law. All his schooling came from other lawyers and Blackstone.

Jackson spent a good deal of his time at the cockfights and horse races; he looked like he was not going to amount to anything. He loved that wild side of life so much. People who knew him at that time thought he didn't have a serious enough mien to be a lawyer—certainly never to be a judge or anything like that.

As a young lawyer, he went up to Jonesboro, in what was to become Tennessee. I think he chose it because it was the wildest town in the country. He became a violent rival of John Sevier, the pioneer, soldier, and first governor of Tennessee. The Sevier people were always getting into fights with the Jackson people. Jackson challenged a lot of people to duels and actually killed a few of them.

Jackson was staying in a small hotel which still stands there in Jonesboro. He was ill. A bunch of the Sevier people came to tar and feather him, and the hotelkeeper warned him they were coming, and told him to get out the back door, get away.

Jackson said, "No, hand me my pistols."

He wrote out a message and sent it out, to the effect that,

Mr. Jackson is awaiting the pleasure of anybody that wants to come in.

Nobody went in.

He was that kind of man. The average Southerner felt when Jackson was elected that the common people finally had their man in, and everything would be all right. This Southern appreciation for populists and demagogues has followed right down to our day.

Why was the word "damn" always put before "Yankee"? Well, Yankees and Southerners never did have anything in common. The history is well known; the North was commercial, the South agricultural. The conflict goes way back, before the Civil War, before the Revolution. Southerners and Northerners didn't have anything in common even then.

It wasn't easy to get from one place to the other. I'm always amazed to read that the best way to get from Boston to Philadelphia in Colonial times was by sea. To go farther south was really difficult. It was inhumanly difficult for George Washington to get from Philadelphia back to his home in Virginia. Georgia, the thirteenth colony, might as well have been on another planet. It was easier to go west after they built the National Road.

But try to go South, and you had a rough time. There was no U.S. Highway 1. Everybody who made trips by road in those days described the roads with horror. I have a ten-foot shelf of books about traveling around America (as you might expect, given my own wandering), and every time I come upon an old travel book, I find it lingers on the subject of the roads.

The National Road, finally, went all the way to Illinois. Travel writers of the day said it was as fine a highway as any in Europe—an Appian Way of the New World.

Charles Dickens made a grumpy trip around America, complaining about nearly everything he saw, but he was impressed by that highway.

I remember John Adams's letter to Abigail about what he thought of Edward Rutledge, the South Carolina delegate to the Continental

Congress. He said Rutledge was "totally vain, totally empty"—you know, a Southerner. He believed that Rutledge, and by extension most of his fellow Southerners, were all style, with no substance at all. The fact that the two of them could agree on this one thing—that the nation had to break with Britain—is impressive to me. It was the one, fundamental thing that they could agree on.

The South was committed to make the break, even though much of its commerce, the cotton trade, depended on England. States like New York hung back, but the South was ready for a free country. It was that independent streak showing itself again.

That streak lay dormant through Jackson's presidency, but as the country grew and the differences between South and North became more evident, it revived as an ember, then as a flame. We must remember that the men who started the Civil War were the sons of men who fought the Revolution, so the concept of a break for independence, defended with guns, was not as foreign to them as it is to us now.

Robert E. Lee was the first man, I suppose, to be a purely *Southern* hero. I knew all about the exploits of Lee, and Stonewall Jackson, and J.E.B. Stuart, and Nathan Bedford Forrest. I don't think many people think of Lee as a hero in the South anymore—unless you go back to the places where he lived and still is revered. Lee's father was a famous man, Light-Horse Harry Lee, a compatriot of George Washington who ended his life in disgrace, up to his ears in debt. But if you visit Stratford Hall on the Northern Neck of Virginia, where he was born, the historical-society ladies will still argue the case with you. They'll tell you that Light-Horse Harry fell into debt not because he was a wild speculator and careless with his money, but because he was excessively generous and lost his fortune to bad debts.

I once spent a night in Lee's room at Washington and Lee University, with his grandfather clock going *click! clock! click! clock!* all night from across the room. Of course I didn't dare stop the damned thing so I could sleep. I was afraid to touch it.

It's true that Lee was a brilliant soldier, the best in the Civil War in the estimation of most people. But after the surrender at Appomattox, he became something more—the embodiment of the Lost Cause. In all the legend making, the man who was Lee has been all but forgotten.

It was his peculiar good fortune to have a most formidable biographer, Douglas Southall Freeman, who gave us a classic four-volume study which has cast the legend in stone for all time. Freeman cataloged at endless length not only the campaigns that made Lee a hero; he dutifully listed in his index nearly every quality inherent in the man, a long list that begins with "Audacity" and "Boldness" and runs all the way through "Urge to Excel" and "Wisdom."

In that way, Lee became for several generations of Southern youth not a man but a myth, a noble exemplar of all that was good and true and worthy in the Southern character. It's easy to imagine that Lee, if he had lived to read Freeman's *Lee*, would have nearly perished of embarrassment.

The legend extended even to Lee's famous horse, Traveller. When Traveller died, he was stuffed and mounted for display in a glass box at

Unveiling the monument to General Robert E. Lee at Richmond, Virginia, in 1890.

135

Washington and Lee, where he stood, crumbling, for decades. At last, not too many years ago, it occurred to someone to give Traveller a decent burial, not far from the crypt of his master. A lady present in the chapel that day opened all the chapel windows and played "Dixie" to mark the occasion. So one legend, at least, was laid to a comfortable rest.

Of heroes, the war gave the South plenty. Of villains, certainly the most notorious was the Union general Ben ("Spoons") Butler, so named by the infuriated ladies of New Orleans after he confiscated their silverware as head of the Union occupation force. (He was also known as Beast Butler; he was not much of a general, but he knew how to outrage an occupied citizenry.)

He was a genuinely bad man, and would have been a bad man whether Northerner or Southerner.

Carl Sandburg told a story about Butler. It seems Lincoln's secretary, John Hay, came in and said he believed Butler was the only man in the Army who would be dangerous if he ever had political power.

As Hay wrote it in his diary, Lincoln said, "Yes, he is like Jim Jett's brother. Jim used to say that his brother was the damndest scoundrel that ever lived, but in the infinite mercy of Providence he was also the damndest fool." That providential characteristic has brought down a lot of demagogues.

In my mind, General William Tecumseh Sherman is and always will be the number one villain of the South. In 1976, during the Bicentennial, I went along the route of Sherman's march from Atlanta to the sea. I found people in Georgia who still hate him, who were still willing to talk bitterly about him. You can still see some signs of his march. You have to look, but those lonely chimneys are still standing there, where houses used to be. The Southerners named those things "Sherman's Sentinels."

Sherman attacked and burned people's homes, and it was precisely that which caused people to hate him so. Oh, how unnecessary it was. Why burn the homes of innocent families? Why do that? Of course, at the time, it seemed to Sherman the only choice, like dropping the bomb on Hiroshima. The war had to be won. It was far, far later, many years after the war, when Sherman was thinking back, that he said, "War is hell."

The unlucky Georgians who lived along his path in 1864 already had found out about that.

I belonged briefly to a fraternity at Chapel Hill. They kept the records of everybody who'd ever been a member. I remember going up to the secret room, where they kept all these records, handwritten. And in the book they showed me where they write a line or two about what happened to you in your life, and when you died. In the class of 1863, there were about seven boys in the fraternity. Two years later, six of them were dead. Those six boys were going to be the leaders of North Carolina. They were the college generation, and that generation was decimated. "Decimated," though, isn't the word, because that just means the death of one in ten.

There are plenty of wretched stories that came out of the Civil War; there were also plenty of examples of kindness to the enemy. But the great bitterness came after the defeat, when it became apparent that many Northerners were determined to grind the South down, to keep the heel of the boot on the South. The United States treated Japan far better after

World War II than the North treated the South after the Civil War.

Remember the decision of Grant to give Lee's defeated soldiers their horses because they would need them for the spring plowing? That was the way the war ended: as a decent settlement between two honorable men.

As historian Bruce Catton put it: "Because of what happened when he and Grant at last met, Lee when he left Appomattox—a paroled soldier without an army—rode straight into legend, and he took his people with him. The legend became a saving grace. The cause that had failed became The Lost Cause, larger than life, taking on color and romance as the years passed, remembered with pride and with heart-ache but never again leading to bloodshed. Civil wars have had worse endings than this."

This graceful conclusion was symbolic of the way things might have been after the war. But things went terribly wrong, and it harmed the country for all the rest of that century, and right up into the Depression days. It took another war—World War II—to bring the South back from the Civil War.

It would have helped if Abraham Lincoln had lived, of course. He was filled with wisdom, and his compassion for the South had made itself felt since the middle of the war. But a great leader was pretty hard to come by right after the war, and that is what the country so greatly needed—a healing leader with a magnanimous spirit. Lincoln had the spirit and the understanding, and he was ready to try to bring us together. He had already talked a good deal about what had to be done quickly.

I suspect Lee would have been a hero to me, if I had come up a little earlier. But we've slipped away from heroes. I think it's probably good that we have outgrown this old business of "My granddaddy rode and fought with Wade Hampton, and I'd shoot a Yankee quicker than I'd stomp a snake." The Civil War's finally over, I believe.

I think the day has finally come when the South's heroes are the heroes of everyone else. I think most people in the South would now acknowledge that Lincoln was one of our greatest Presidents. That bitterness of the past is mostly gone, except in remote pockets.

But after the war, and after Lincoln's assassination, there wasn't much room for heroes in the South. There were only scoundrels there, for a time.

Huey Long surely was the next hero. Of course, thinking people here and elsewhere in the country were as appalled by Huey Long as they had been by Andrew Jackson, and even more so. There was in Long also the streak of the demagogue. He and others like him were popular heroes, but there was good reason to think of them as dangerous. Inciting the mob and all that—they were glad to do it. They were specialists in it, as a matter of fact.

I'll tell you who became a hero in the South, in my memory: Roosevelt. He's the hero I remember. He wasn't FDR, or "the President." He was Roosevelt; there was only one. I don't remember any criticism of him at all. People had no faith in any of his recent predecessors, and in Roosevelt they suddenly found someone to put all their faith in.

REA, WPA, CCC, and the fireside chats; it just seemed that finally there was a President in office who cared about the common man. This fellow was a man of the people. It didn't matter where he'd come from or that he spoke with a different accent. He was on our side. He was there to help.

Franklin Delano Roosevelt (lower right, in car, waving hat) visits Beauvoir, near Biloxi, Mississippi, in 1937, where Jefferson Davis spent the last years of his life.

These women of Louisville
have little doubt about whom
they favor in the mayoral
race of 1921.

So was Eleanor Roosevelt. People would write to her about the smallest problems in their lives, and she always made an effort to respond.

Of course, this admiration wasn't universal. There were businesspeople in the South who felt, as did some of those in the North, that Roosevelt was going to bring ruin with his complex schemes. But the rank and file of Southerners admired Roosevelt more than anyone else in my time.

Sergeant York was a great hero between the wars. The movie came out when I was a little boy, and I grew up in awe of him.

Southerners always admired people who were in the war. Any war. Harry Caudill of Whitesburg, Kentucky, told me that all the candidates running for sheriff were making speeches one day, on the courthouse steps. All these guys came up, one by one, and recounted (modestly) how they had been wounded in the war. It was about the only qualification any of them had. And this one man said, "As you know, I wasn't wounded in the war. I was 4-F. But I need the job bad. And I *am* the worst ruptured man in Letcher County."

I believe that man won.

Even George Wallace was, to some people in the South, one of the last heroes. His stand against integration in the schoolhouse door was much admired by many people. And at the same time, to other people, Martin Luther King was becoming a hero. Dr. King lost his life in the struggle, but George Wallace ended up embracing many of the things Dr. King fought for. I leave it to you to decide who won the battle between them.

You can't come along and say, "Listen, I know what's best" and expect to get elected in the South. You always have to say, "I'm just as common as you are," and that's how you win.

When I was a young reporter covering Earl Long's troubles as governor of Louisiana, Long found himself committed to a mental hospital. I was one of a pack of reporters chasing the Governor outside the court the day he won his freedom. I stayed right beside the Governor with my microphone—he knew me, so he didn't seem to object—and I was muscling in, shouting questions at him. I heard the Governor's chief bodyguard say to his men, "Get that one," and they all decided he meant me.

I was roundhoused, blindsided. There's a wonderful UPI picture of me, snapped at the moment I went over backward.

The next thing I knew, I was on my back being trampled by the rest of the herd. But I was determined to get the story. Long and his girlfriend, the stripper Blaze Starr, disappeared somewhere in Louisiana. My cameraman and I tracked him down to a tiny roadhouse motel outside of Covington, on Lake Pontchartrain. It was a motor court with no air-conditioning, just little screened doors that opened to the parking lot.

I knocked on the door, and Miss Starr came up. I shouted past her, "Governor, are you in there?" He said he was, but in his underwear. So I interviewed him through the screen door.

He said he was tired of the hubbub, the politics, and the press, and he wanted to get close to his people. Just to do some plain thing. So he had gone to a hardware store and purchased two items: a watermelon and a hoe. I suppose he had in mind going out to plant watermelon seeds.

There's something exclusively Southern about that kind of politician.

The Southerner certainly suffered, in my memory, from an inferiority complex. He felt that opportunity existed in the North, not in the South; that the North was on top and the South was on the bottom. There's still a little bit of it even today.

In Atlanta's race to become a great metropolis, you can see a bit of that pride—"Look, we're a Southern city"—that dates back to the war.

We're over it, now, I believe—and not least because so many Northerners have found the South so charming. The South now attracts Northerners like honey attracts flies. When I said, in the old days, that I was from North Carolina, people would say, "Yeah, I was at Fort Bragg," or Camp Lejeune, or Fort Rucker, or Biloxi. They'd been based in the South.

But now, the Northerners' experience of the South is much different. They go to Orlando, or Myrtle Beach, or New Orleans, or Charleston. And they sense this rare openness and friendliness; they can't get over it. They don't treat you on the Jersey Shore the way they treat you in Myrtle Beach. Northerners have discovered the South, and they love it.

They like the food; they like the "ambience." We Southerners, of course, look on all this with a sort of bemusement. And there are regrettable elements to it, as well, especially in the vacation communities. They're building at least one Tara in Atlanta now, and there's talk of a second. Seems that people attend conventions, and the one thing on the top of the list they want to see is Tara. It does no good to remind them that *Gone with the Wind* is fiction, and that Tara never existed.

Dallas has Southfork Ranch, which is the site of the popular fictional TV show set there. It's the biggest tourist attraction in the area, and it's all based on some California screenwriter's idea of Texas.

The place where my parents live on Currituck Sound in North Carolina is a community where a lot of Northerners retire. And there is a certain tension there, at least between my mother, who knows the South in her bones, and these people who keep making the discovery that Southern food is good and that Southerners aren't all hillbillies. They irritate my mother no end, those people who look on the South as some strange and different place.

I frequently visit the mountains of North Carolina, and I'm somewhat disturbed by what's happening there. People are coming from the North to build their planned communities around lakes. These developments have gates and gatehouses and guards. There is *that* mountain North Carolina, and then there's the mountain North Carolina that's always been there, and the two have not mixed at all. The people who've always been there have become groundkeepers of the estates, or caddies at the golf courses. The newcomers may occasionally do business at one of the country stores, but not much business, because some Northern company has built a shopping center in there behind the gates.

Everybody seems to approve of it, though, except me and my mother. This "progress" has brought money in where it was needed. But it seems to me it has also brought a new class structure, a new division based on money and status. I'm awfully glad the whole South hasn't gone that way. There may even be a place or two left where people don't watch "Dallas."

"The politics of the Old South was a theater for the play of the purely personal, the purely romantic, and the purely hedonistic. It was an arena wherein one great champion confronted another or a dozen, and sought to outdo them in rhetoric and splendid gesturing. It swept back the loneliness of the land, it brought men together under torches, it filled them with the contagious power of the crowd, it unleashed emotion and set it to leaping and dancing, it caught the very meanest man up out of his own tiny legend into the gorgeous fabric of the legend of this or that great hero."

—W. J. Cash, *The Mind of the South*

Cash, that great observer of our politics, would have been the first to note that it took a certain kind of man to sustain the public's interest in such a "play of the purely personal." And many of the greatest were men (and women) of such strong personal conviction that they could not help acting as lightning rods for one cause or another. Lucky for us there were men such as Chief Justice John Marshall, who kept a steady hand on the tiller for thirty-four years, and Henry Clay, who helped hold a fractured nation together with the passion of his oratory.

Above: John Marshall of Virginia served as chief justice of the Supreme Court from 1801 to 1835.

Left: Roger Taney was chief justice when the Dred Scott decision was handed down in 1857.

Right: Harriet Tubman, a chief engineer on the Underground Railroad, stands at the far left with some of the slaves she helped to free.

Above: Members of the Women's Christian Temperance Union display their support for prohibition at a Bainbridge, Georgia, parade in 1923.

Left: Woodrow Wilson appointed Kentuckian Louis Brandeis to the Supreme Court in 1916.

The Orators' Corner: While vice president, South Carolina's John C. Calhoun (above) was a forceful promoter of states' rights. Ex-slave Frederick Douglass (above right) was a radical abolitionist who stated his position in militant rhetoric. Henry Clay of Kentucky (right) thrice failed to capture the presidency but had success in initiating the Compromise of 1850 and forestalling the split of the Union.

Below: Supreme Court Justice John Harlan of Kentucky dissented in the case of Plessy v. Ferguson, which established the doctrine of separate but equal facilities for blacks.

Above: Separate but equal facilities in action: a Memphis bus station in 1943.

Right: Waiting for the courthouse to open in a North Carolina town (1897).

A powerful Texas triumvirate: John Nance Garner (above) moved fr[om] Speaker of the House to [v]ice president, under FDR in 1933. Cactus Jack's protégé, Sam Rayburn (above center), filled the Speaker's slot from 1940[–]1961. In turn, Rayburn played mentor to Lyndon Johnson (above right), w[ho] went from Senate majori[ty] leader to vice president in 1960.

Left: Former Alabama KKK member Hugo Black became a great Supreme Court justice during his thirty-four years on the bench.

Above: At the Scopes trial in Dayton, Tennessee, in 1925, Clarence Darrow argued for the right to teach evolution.

Below: Richmond suffragettes campaign for the Nineteenth Amendment in 1916.

Above: "Kingfish" Huey Long ruled the state of Louisiana with an iron hand, first as governor, then as senator. He woul[d] have been Roosevelt's strongest competition for 1936 Democratic presidential nomination had he not been assassinated in 1935.

Left: The first woman admitted to the Kentucky [bar was] Sophonisba Breckinridge[.]

It's hard to believe that Huey Long and Martin Luther King could both be heroes in the South in the same century, but they were. We've always been partial to populists—just the suggestion that "I'm one of you" was a good way to get elected. Lyndon Johnson learned it from Sam Rayburn, who learned it from "Cactus Jack" Garner. This goes down to the courthouse level, too.

Above: Senator Theodore Bilbo of Mississippi was a rabble-rouser in the Huey Long tradition.

Left: Adept at employing fear as a weapon, the Ku Klux Klan used cross burnings as a device of intimidation.

Below: The 101st Airborne Division stands by as Little Rock High School is integrated in 1957.

Above: Miriam Ferguson delivers her inauguration speech as governor of Texas in 1925. After her husband, "Pa," was evicted from the governor's office, "Ma" ran in his stead.

Right: Rebecca Felton, the first woman appointed to the U.S. Senate, also followed in the footsteps of a politician husband.

Left: Rosa Parks, after her arrest for participating in the Montgomery bus boycott in 1956.

Hardly anybody at the time would have believed that the convulsions of the civil rights movement would lead the South into a new and better day, but it has. It took the bravery of common people, and the ringing words of great leaders. Rosa Parks decided to keep her seat on a city bus in Montgomery, Alabama, and the shock resounded around the nation. A group of black college students in Greensboro decided to sit at a lunch counter until they were served, and within weeks, students all over the country were following their lead. Martin Luther King, Jr., stood before a great sea of people and announced his dream in the most effective political speech of twentieth century America. A nation was ignited. Collisions would follow. But things would never again be the same.

Above: Howard Baker of Tennessee confers with chairman Sam Ervin of North Carolina at the Senate Watergate hearings in 1973.

Left: Estes Kefauver became a television star when he headed the Senate committee investigating organized crime in 1950-51. His trademark, borrowed from fellow Tennessean Davy Crockett, was the famous coonskin cap.

Above: Rev. Martin Luther King, Jr., made his stirring "I Have a Dream" speech in Washington in 1963.

Below: President Jimmy Carter with Rev. Martin Luther King, Sr., in 1976.

Left: Professor John Langston founded the Law School at Howard University in 1868.

Far left: Students from North Carolina A&T State University in the first sit-in at the Greensboro Woolworth's lunch counter in 1960.

Left: A loyal supporter hugs a picture of Alabama governor George Wallace at a Spirit of America festival in 1974.

Right: Former congresswoman Barbara Jordan was appointed professor of public affairs at the University of Texas.

149

*Curb exchange, 1940: Although the grass roots had been
paved over around the courthouse of Versailles, Kentucky, citizens
congregated for consideration of matters great and small.*

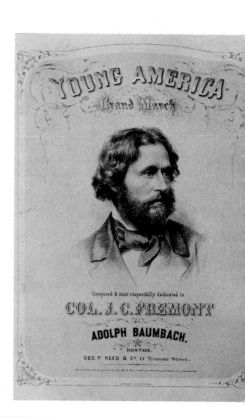

Appointed by President Jefferson, Virginians Meriwether Lewis (far left) and William Clark (left) pioneered a trail to the northwest in 1804-06. Frontiersman Daniel Boone (above, circa 1832) was once tried for treason due to his Tory sympathies. Georgian John Charles Frémont (right) helped win California in the war with Mexico and ran for the presidency, unsuccessfully, in 1856.

What a restless, energetic nation it must have been. The East was barely settled, and certainly not yet tamed, when explorers began to reach out to the West. Daniel Boone blazed the Wilderness Road and set the example for those who would become legends in America. He was widely held to be polite, good-humored, and modest, as well as one terrific warrior. It was Thomas Jefferson who sent two young Virginians, Meriwether Lewis and William Clark, on a journey to explore the Louisiana Territory that he would later purchase from the French. They ultimately went all the way to the Pacific. Their mission was not so different from today's space program, both intended to widen the boundaries of our maps and our minds. Stephen Austin's life—born in Virginia, raised in Missouri, his greatest glory established in Texas—reflects all the great migrations of the Southern people. John C. Frémont, "the Pathmaker," carved trails into Oregon and California that made possible the ultimate move westward. But people who most wanted the wide open spaces were usually content to stop in Texas, where you could find a three-million-acre ranch (the XIT) sprawling over ten counties.

Virginian Stephen F. Austin (at top), "the Father of Texas."
Kentuckian Judge Roy Bean dispensed justice and cold beer in Langtry, Texas (left),
named for Lillie Langtry—"the Jersey Lilly"—a star of the 1880s.
Above, cowboys wearing slickers take a break on the huge XIT Ranch in Texas (1898).

Americans were too restless, too adventurous, and too ambitious to remain confined in the East. Southerners had these qualities, and were born to lead the drive. Westward expansion and our various experiments in empire building were inevitable. Sam Houston, a Virginian, became the greatest hero of the fight to claim Texas—his army avenged the Alamo massacre, crushed Santa Anna at San Jacinto, and he became the first president of the Lone Star Republic. Another Virginian, Winfield Scott, took Mexico City and resolved that conflict forever. John Tyler Morgan wheeled and dealed for a canal across Central America; William Gorgas's great strides in controlling malaria and yellow fever made it possible.

A group of San Antonio cowboys, before and after being recruited in a
bar by Teddy Roosevelt for his Rough Riders, 1898.

Left: Soldiers practicing with howitzers at Fort Story in Virginia Beach, circa 1917. Fort Story was so heavily armed that it was known as the American Gibraltar.

Above: At Westminster Abbey to decorate Britain's Tomb of the Unknown Soldier in 1921, Missouri General John ("Black Jack") Pershing inspects the Guard of Honor.

Below: Eighteen-year-old Tommy Hitchcock went from the polo fields of Palm Beach to the Lafayette Escadrille in France.

Above left: A Texas soldier wounded at Ville sur Tier in 1918.

Left: Marine aviation cadets in Miami.

Southerners always admired
people who were in the war. Any war.
When the first modern, "total"
war broke out among the nations of
Europe, the South leaped to organize
regiments, to offer its sons and its land for
the training of troops in new styles of
combat. Most of the pilots who flew in
World War I were trained in Florida,
since it had the largest number of flying
days each year. Southern "welcome
home" celebrations were elaborate affairs;
the South, as always, was eager to
acknowledge the heroism of its warriors.
Corporal Alvin C. York became the
nation's greatest hero. When a German
platoon lured his soldiers into a trap
with a false surrender, York used a rifle
and then a pistol to round up 132
prisoners single-handedly. The movie
about his life came out when I was a
little boy, and I grew up in awe of him. But
World War I marked something
darker as well—an end to innocence, a
final burial of the gentleman's code of war.

Top left: Calisthenics, complete with gas masks, at an Air Corps basic training center at Miami Beach, Florida, 1943. Top right: A soldier home on leave in Brown Summit, North Carolina, 194 Above: Nattily and nautically attired, the Nance family in convoy at Fort Pierce, Florida, 1942. Right: Audie Murphy of Farmersville, Texas. The awards won and worn by the most decorated hero of WW II include the Congressional Medal.

One flag in the window for each son in service, a mother stands on her porch in Plaquemines Parish, Louisiana, 1943. At right: Lt. Gen. "Howling Mad" Smith, USMC, of Alabama, in command at Iwo Jima; Maj. Gen. Lemuel Shepherd, USMC, of Virginia, led assault on Okinawa in 1945; Florida's "Vinegar Joe" Stilwell, chief of staff to Chiang Kai-shek of China; Oveta Culp Hobby of Texas commanded the WAC.

The bombing of Pearl Harbor on December 7, 1941, called America to arms and once again Southerners stepped forward. The rebel yell was heard from Anzio to the Philippines, where a detail of Texans (at right) hoisted the Lone Star banner. Good fighters of all ranks, the war's most decorated hero was a Southerner. Revitalized by the war, the South, however, paid a great price in giving many of its best.

At right: Gen. Douglas MacArthur of Little Rock helped turn defeat into victory in the Pacific. He later governed postwar Japan. MacArthur's record at West Point was second only to Robert E. Lee's; Lt. Gen. Courtney Hodges of Georgia, one of Eisenhower's commanders in Europe; Adm. Chester Nimitz of Texas, victor at the battle of Midway; Lt. Gen. Leonard Gerow of Virginia, among first Americans to reenter Paris in 1945.

There seems to have been no generation of Southerners that did not know war. The men who led the armies of the Civil War were the sons and grandsons of those who fought in the Revolution. And how many soldiers of this century grew up hearing tales of ancient battle from old men who actually fought in the Civil War, the Spanish-American, the "Great War," the "Big War"? There is something in the Southern character which makes us quick to take up arms in defense of rights, real or perceived. War is considered not only a duty, but an opportunity and (at least between wars) an adventure. David Glasgow Farragut, who left the South to fight for the Union, achieved his rare sort of immortality not by his crucial conquests of New Orleans and Mobile, but by the dash and bravado with which he carried them off. Alabama's Richmond Hobson led a suicide mission in Cuba, and survived. The South cheers its heroes, mourns its losses, but never shrinks from its duty. That is a tradition down here.

A lad of military mien snaps to attention for the photographer in Heber Springs, Arkansas. At left, General-to-be Douglas MacArthur as a 16-year-old cadet at West Texas Military Academy, 1896. Below: First in his class of 1889 at Annapolis, Richmond Pearson Hobson was a hero of the Spanish-American War. Right: A military school in Montgomery, Alabama, 1900, is not quite uniformly outfitted. Note ad for gun store on butt of wooden rifle.

Above: WW II hero Chester Nimitz with his grandfather, a Civil War veteran (circa 1910). Left: Tennessee's David Farragut, a Union admiral, saw battle at Mobile Bay in 1864. Right: Gen. William Westmoreland of South Carolina was commander in Vietnam until 1968.

Left: A line of wing walkers, Houston (circa 1920).

Right: North Carolina's "Tiny" Broadwick reins in after a demonstration jump (circa 1913).

Below: Virginian Richard Byrd received a ticker-tape parade and Congressional Medal for his flight over North Pole, 1926.

They may have been Yankees, Orville and Wilbur, but they traveled to a lonely, windswept beach in North Carolina to try out their rickety invention. Ever since, the South has been a good place to take flight. When America decided to go to the moon, NASA went to a beach in Florida (and decided to run things from Houston, a decision heavily influenced by Texan Lyndon Johnson). Air shows and wing walkers still bring them out by the thousands all over the South, and a launch at Cape Canaveral is an event of national importance.

Left: Fort Sam Houston in San Antonio, Texas, 1912. In the sky are a Wright "C" flyer and a Curtiss pusher biplane.

Right: Mission control at Johnson Space Center in Houston, 1985.

Below: A space shuttle launch at Kennedy Space Center in Florida, 1981.

ght: Claire Chennault Texas, leader of the ing Tigers during rld War II.

ow: Test pilot Chuck ger of West Virginia ke the sound barrier 1947.

Left: Robert Crippen of Texas flew in the first space shuttle, Columbia, in 1981.

Below: Ronald McNair of Lake City, South Carolina, died in the explosion of the space shuttle Challenger in 1986.

163

Above: David Marshall ("Carbine") Williams invented the M1 carbine in the early forties, while in a North Carolina prison.

Right: The carbine in action in World War II.

Left: Jim Bowie of Louisiana designed the knife which bears his name.

Professor Richard Gatling of North Carolina developed the rapid-fire Gatling gun in 1862. He later became the first president of the American Association of Inventors and Manufacturers.

There was no end to the mechanical ingenuity of the South. Since we were the agricultural heartland of the nation before the Civil War, it was only natural that Cyrus McCormick came from Virginia. His invention changed life forever. Some scholars see the beginning of the end of slavery as the day McCormick patented this monumental labor saver. Then it was only a matter of time until machines would become more valuable than men in the fields. Some of our other inventions were more deadly: the Bowie knife, the Gatling gun, the carbine. It's worth noting that some variation of each of these inventions is still in use today.

Virginian Cyrus McCormick patented his reaper in 1834. He made his invention highly profitable by pioneering the installment plan as a means of purchase.

165

The famous race of the Robert E. Lee *and the* Natchez *in 1870 (above) masked a personal duel between captains.*
The Lee *won and set the New Orleans to St. Louis speed record for steamboats which stands to this day. On a more*
relaxed voyage, lunch is served aboard the St. Joseph (above right, circa 1895). A far cry from the
flat-bottomed side-wheeler, the aircraft carrier Enterprise *(right) is launched at Newport News, Virginia, in 1936.*

Only in the old South could a steamboat be bred and trained for speed like a horse, decorated like the most fanciful of wedding cakes, staffed by the best chefs and servants and entertainers, and set adrift up the mighty Mississip' to do nothing more complicated than take passengers from one place to another. Mark Twain knew they were an endangered species when he wrote about them so well. Today's riverboats survive and thrive, but not quite so elegantly.

Two views of the High Bridge, which carries a railroad over the Kentucky River near Wilmore—a close-up with strollers and, at right, a longer view with puffing engine and payload, 1907. Below: Two small boys pose with crew of gleaming Engine No. 16 of the Florida Railway & Navigation Company.

It was a time of pure optimism, a time when people could look at scenes such as this and still fervently believe the oil would last forever. Oil was an oozy black nuisance to early settlers in Texas and Oklahoma; it got in their water wells, and not until the mid-nineteenth century did anyone think to use it as a fuel. Once that happened, though, the boom was on— incredible gushers, wild races to obtain leases, cheating and killing, fortunes made overnight. The landscapes of some awfully lonesome spots were transformed into bizarre citylike skylines, like that of Humble, Texas, where the mighty giant that became Exxon was born.

"Where the rain never falls and the sun never shines,
Oh, it's dark as a dungeon way down in the mines."

How else but as a dungeon could a man describe it—climbing into a hole every morning before the sun's up, spending the whole day hammering, sweating, digging, lifting, in fear of every rumble and odd smell. Breathing the coal dust so long that it smells like fresh air. Leaving each evening after the sun has already gone down. Mining provided a living, but only barely, for many men in regions where the soil was so poor that it would grow nothing but rocks. Mining started a legend, of heroic men slaving away for their next dollar, that is not far from the truth. Mining isn't a job I would want to do.

Preparing for a blast, men and equipment cast eerie shadows in a salt dome at Avery Island, Louisiana (1949). Disappointing news is posted for coal miners in Harlan County, Kentucky (above, 1946). Gold miners J. Wadsworth and R. M. Miller, photographed in 1882 (above right) at the Rudisill Mine, over which the city of Charlotte, North Carolina, now stands.

At work in the South's oldest industry. Horses, oxen, men, and mules haul logs at the Lathrop-Hatten Lumber Company in St. Clair County, Alabama. This picture was taken a few years before Southern lumbering hit its high, cutting sixteen-billion board feet of yellow pine in 1909. Above: Two lumberjacks, tall and lean as the trees they fell, in southeast Louisiana in the same decade.

Taking advantage of good weather, a broom factory moves outdoors. Carlisle County, Kentucky (circa 1900).

Many Southerners followed King Cotton into the textile mills and factories. Above, in the White Oak Mills of Greensboro, North Carolina, men attend beaming frames on which thread is straightened for looming (circa 1907). At left, in an unusual photograph taken at what was probably the Avondale Mill, women are interrupted at work by Brother Bryan of the Third Presbyterian Church of Birmingham. One of the best-known clerics of the area, he regularly preached at the workplace to police, firemen, and, as here, mill workers. How the owners felt about the diversion of workers' attention from matters at hand is difficult to divine.

There can hardly be any confusion about the nature of this business in San Marcos, Texas, 1940. At right, the ultimate auto repair advertises Mueller's in Louisville.

MUELLER AUTO REPAIR

FRANCK & PAYNE STS.

"Service that Satisfies"

HIGH. 2987

180

One family's flagship bogs down in an attempted river crossing on a trip in the Ozarks near Potosi, Washington County, Missouri, circa 1912.

Outside the post office of Belle Glade, Florida, in 1940, kids from a migratory labor camp pose with "The Boogie Woogie." Below, Bill Smith of Roane County, Tennessee, poses with his 1968 Chevelle racer.

It's tempting to become nostalgic when you remember that fancy old hand-operated gasoline pump, the twenty-cent gallon of gas, the kind of service you got at the stations in town and along the country roads. But let's not forget the cantankerous hand-cranked engines, the pothole-filled roads, the lack of streetlighting, and other dubious joys of the days when a trip in a car was still an adventure.

*A posse of Houston car salesmen, photographed about 1938, affects the boots
and cowboy hats of a horsier past. At left, brewers of Lone Star
Lager Beer convene (1920) in San Antonio, while the crew of a Louisville
moving company (below, 1925) poses before its truck that boasts
"The World Moves—So Do We." Overleaf: A well-bibbed Texas Bankers Association
tour group stops in New York for a banquet given by shipowner Samuel Morse (1907).*

From the wealth of images that survives, it seems that almost any time a group of people got together for the purpose of conducting business, or to congratulate themselves on business well conducted, they took a break, went outside, lined up, and had their picture made. It was only a moment in the lives of most of these men; we may assume that it was just another day's work for the photographer called in to record the moment. But whether a company portrait wound up in a dusty frame on the wall at headquarters or found its way onto a page like this one, it is a visual time capsule—a record, almost always serious, of the way companies viewed themselves at their best.

The Southern tycoon was typically a man who had learned the value of a dollar because his family didn't have many. Then, when he came on the inspired idea of his life (most of us are lucky to have one) he had a flair for selling it. Harland Sanders married a good recipe for fried chicken to the fledgling idea of franchising. Henry Morrison Flagler made his fortune in the oil business, but he's remembered for opening Florida to tourists. Asa Candler didn't concoct Coca-Cola, but he knew a good product when he tasted it, and he had the good sense to buy the formula one year after John Pemberton invented it. Howard Hughes's incalculable fortune came not from a single inspiration—the *Hercules,* a.k.a. "The Spruce Goose," was not particularly inspired—but from a lifetime full of them. Today's tycoons, among them H. Ross Perot, the Hunt brothers, and merger-maker T. Boone Pickens, are distinguished by their willingness to take giant risks without regard for conventional wisdom.

North Carolina tobacco tycoons and philanthropists Benjamin and James Duke on the boardwalk at Atlantic City (1920s). Right and below: Secretive Texas billionaire Howard Hughes's interests ranged from oil to movies. One of his ventures was the 1947 flying boat, "The Spruce Goose," named for its basic material: plywood.

Top left and right: Texas oil baron H. L. Hunt and his son Lamar. Above: Kentucky Fried Chicken's dapper Colonel Sanders. Right: Ross Perot, whose fortune-making EDS is now part of General Motors, takes to horse in 1970.

Asa Griggs Candler, the Atlanta pharmacist who made Coca-Cola an empire, is shown here (above, third from left) with employees, 1899.
Left: Tennessee-born Jesse Jones, a Texas real estate wizard, owned the Houston Chronicle. Shown here about 1927, he later served FDR as secretary of commerce.
Right: Railroad magnate Henry Flagler and ladies, circa 1908.

To me, a large part of growing up was all baseball. I was an absolute baseball fanatic. Played, every day after school. Listened to the radio, every game. Saturdays, went to minor league games—distinctly minor league. But that didn't matter to me. I knew every detail about every player. Wherever you lived, no matter what school you went to or what you did for a living, there was a baseball team playing nearby. The smell of a catcher's mitt was universal, as were the crack of a good hit, the smell of a hot dog, the dust on your britches. Many of the game's greatest players made their first catches on sandlots on warm spring evenings in the South, with teams like the one from Cedar Grove, North Carolina. The bull pen got its name from a Bull Durham tobacco campaign that paid twenty-five dollars to any hitter who swatted one against the outfield sign.

Top row: A soaring catch by Willie Mays, the "Say, Hey Kid," from Mobile. Johnny Mize of Demorest, Georgia, four-time National League home run champ. "Mr. Cub" Ernie Banks of Dallas. Hall of Famer Rogers Hornsby, native of Winters, Texas. 1944 National League batting champ, Dixie Walker of Villa Rica, Georgia. Alvin Dark of Comanche, Oklahoma.

Second row: Twice American League batting champ, Luke Appling of High Point, North Carolina. Willie McCovey of Mobile, 1969 National League MVP. Shoeless Joe Jackson, of the notorious 1919 Black Sox scandal, from Brandon Mills, South Carolina. All-time home run king, Hank Aaron of Mobile. Dizzy Dean of Lucas, Arkansas, pitched his way into the Hall of Fame.

Third row: Baseball Commissioner "Happy" Chandler reigned from 1945 to 1951. Catcher Jimmy Foxx of Suldersville, Maryland, three-time American League MVP. Ty Cobb of Narrows, Georgia, still holds the American League career record for stolen bases. Jackie Robinson of Cairo, Georgia, broke baseball's color barrier.

Fourth row: The inimitable windup of Mobile's Satchel Paige. Pitcher Lefty Grove of Lanconing, Maryland, entered the Hall of Fame with three hundred wins. Memphis's Tim McCarver, now a baseball announcer.

Fifth row: Mel Ott of Gretna, Louisiana, led the National League in home runs six times. Enos ("Country") Slaughter of Roxboro, North Carolina. The Sultan of Swat himself, Baltimore's own Babe Ruth. Tris Speaker of Hubbard, Texas.

Sixth row: In 1952, Allie Reynolds of Bethany, Oklahoma, had lowest earned run average. "Catfish" Hunter of Hertford, North Carolina, pitched a perfect game against the Twins in 1968. Bill Terry of Atlanta was the National League batting champ in 1930, with a stunning .401 average.

*Left: Ole Miss
quarterback Archie
Manning.*

*Right: LSU's Billy
Cannon, a great
running back, won the
Heisman Trophy in
1959.*

*Below: The launching of
a dynasty—the first
Alabama football team,
1892.*

*Left: Oklahoma's L
Heath evades a
Kentucky tackle for
big gain in the 1951
Sugar Bowl.*

*Below left:
Oklahoma's Bud
Wilkinson coached
three national
championships.*

*Above: The people fo
whom football is
life-and-death, the f*

*Right: Alabama's Lee
Roy Jordan.*

*Far right: North
Carolina's Charlie
("Choo Choo") Justice.*

*Above right: Duke
students confirm their
high scholastic standing
with a Saturday
afternoon spelling test.*

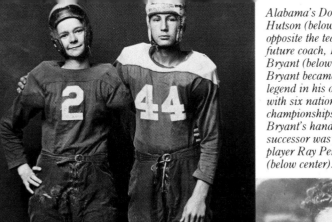

Far left: Army's Doc Blanchard of South Carolina was the 1945 Heisman winner.

Left: 1985 Heisman winner, Auburn's elusive Bo Jackson.

Below: Georgia's Charley Trippi.

Right: Aspiring All-Americans from Arkansas, circa 1942.

Alabama's Don Hutson (below) played opposite the team's future coach, Bear Bryant (below bottom). Bryant became a legend in his own right with six national championships. Bryant's hand-picked successor was former player Ray Perkins (below center).

ove: College
tball's most
orious coach,
die Robinson of
mbling.

ve right:
inging" Sammy
ugh of TCU.

ht: Heisman
ner Herschel
lker of Georgia.

ow: Tuskegee
titute cheerleaders.

August is finished. Time hangs over the landscape like a physical anxiety. The South can only wait and listen for the unstruck chord of College Football. Nowhere is this more true than at the University of Georgia in Athens, as it prepares for an afternoon of reckoning with Auburn in the game that brought major college football to the South in 1892. Think, if you will, on the sheer immensity of Alabama at Tennessee, a rivalry that stands with Texas-Oklahoma—games which Willie Morris has said, "resemble the clashes of contemporary armies." Or have you ever seen Clemson and South Carolina; or any combination of North Carolina and North Carolina State and Duke; or considered the hated alphabetical implications of SMU, TCU, A&M? You will have your own estimation of the great grudge matches, the practiced, old, consecutive vendettas between antique Southern rivals. They increase the appetite for each new college football season.

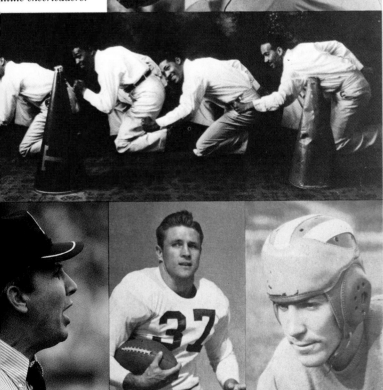

ove: Auburn coach
t Dye.

ove right: SMU's
ak Walker.

ove far right:
nnessee Volunteer
attie Feathers.

ght: In the 1941
gar Bowl,
nnessee lost to
ston College.

Left: A Derby Day race at Churchill Downs shortly before the running of the 1985 Kentucky Derby.

Eddie Arcaro won the Triple Crown on fellow Kentuckian Citation in 1948 (below). Bluegrass native Steve Cauthen (upper right) is a top jockey in both America and England. The winningest rider of all, Texan Willie Shoemaker (right), won the 1986 Kentucky Derby on Kentucky-bred Ferdinand.

Far below: Gentlemen at Churchill Downs find matters at hand more interesting than those afield (circa 1900).

Far right: Richard Singleton with top-hatted trainer Harry. Painted by Edward Troye in 1834.

There is no day quite so elegant as Derby Day at Churchill Downs—the graceful architecture of the grandstand, the carefully groomed grounds, the taste of a mint julep, the echo of thousands singing *"My Old Kentucky Home."* There are plenty of other places in the world to raise and race thoroughbred horses, but as the Queen of England knows, and the great Willie Shoemaker proved on Ferdinand in the 1986 Derby, Kentucky is simply the best.

Above and far right: The scene at the Southern 500 in Darlington, South Carolina. Above right: Congressman William Bankhead is the starter of a three-way race at Alabama's Albertville Fairgrounds in 1929. North Carolina's Richard Petty (right), seven-time NASCAR Grand National Champion. Two other Carolinians, Junior Johnson and Cale Yarborough (second right). Texan A. J. Foyt (third right) won his fourth Indy 500 in 1977.

As soon as somebody brought the automobile South, you can bet some Southern boy got in it and drove it too fast. When he found somebody to race against, and a crowd of his friends and neighbors gathered round to watch, stock car racing was born. Since then, there's been something irresistible about an infield, a tailgate picnic, and the rush of machines at great speed. A. J. Foyt and Richard Petty have proved conclusively that Southern racers aren't all dirt-track-and-snuff boys, but you can find that old-fashioned style any Saturday afternoon at hundreds of tracks across the South.

HOTEL CLARENDON, SEABREEZE, FLA.

Left: A postcard from the Hotel Clarendon in Seabreeze, Florida (circa 1920). Impeccable tennis whites held sway.

Below: Grass court doubles on a groundkeeper's nightmare, at the Mountain Top Hotel in Afton, Virginia (circa 1890).

Right: An Oklahoma quintet (circa 1935).

Below right: Clock golf, a turn-of-the-century fad at the Royal Palm in Miami (1905).

Below far right: Athlete extraordinaire, Babe Didrikson Zaharias of Texas popularized the women's golf tour in the 1940s. She also excelled in basketball, track and field (winning two Olympic gold medals in 1932), and baseball.

The Hotel Clarendon, like many grand resorts across the South, was built to indulge the new passions of a newly mobile upper class—tennis, golf, and automobile racing (the Daytona Speedway was across the street). Some of the playing conditions were a bit rough-hewn at first, a far cry from the fussed-over, manicured courts and greens of modern Southern resorts. You didn't have to be rich to enjoy the game, though, as illustrated by the rather casual Oklahoma quintet (above).

At first, when Southern men began to have enough time to play sports, women were either excluded or relegated to those games considered ladylike. The girls in gym class at Incarnate Word High School were told that proper exercise resulted not only in "graceful movements and dignified bearing," but could also promote "superior intellectual ability." But Southern women, as usual, would not be excluded, even from some of the rough-tough sports played only by men. No one would argue with "Plinky" Topperwein (far right), who, with a .22 rifle at a distance of twenty feet, hit 1,995 out of 2,000 little wood blocks tossed in the air. The elaborately posed fencer at right was most likely a member of a touring company. It's taken a long time, but most barriers are down now, and Southern sportswomen have challenged every record in the book.

San Antonian Gladys Hoffman gets off a good kick (left, 1925). One year later, a gym class in that city executes "Hands behind head—place!" Below, an Anna Held fencing girl poses in Louisville, 1902. At right, Texan sharpshooter "Plinky" Topperwein at the 1904 St. Louis World's Fair.

When aristocrats moved from England to begin new lives in the New World, they brought with them a favorite custom—fox hunting. Dogs and hunters worked in perfect unison to trail a prey that often remained uncaught. The leader of the hunt went ahead with the hounds to find a fox, then signaled with his horn—and the chase was off, over fields and into woods, jumping fences, scrambling through thickets. For those who rode to hounds, it was an unforgettable experience.

The Belle Meade Hunt rides out in Thompson, Georgia (above, 1984), while the Deep Run Hunt Club pauses in central Virginia (below, circa 1900). A riderless horse clears the rail fence in The End of the Hunt *(at left, 1780s, artist unknown). Beautifully poised, a woman (upper left) rides sidesaddle at Castle Hill, Virginia.*

*Left: Two spruced-up Texans, three
trussed bucks, and one surly kid
are snapped between Irvin's ice cream
trucks (circa 1925). Right: A rich
bag of ducks and geese brought to
market in Norfolk, Virginia (1920).
Below, in Frederick County, Maryland
a hunting party lounges at camp . . . n
two men wearing ties (circa 1900).
Far right: A Kentucky woman displays
rifle, powder horn, and beaded belt
(thought to be Laurel County, 1913).*

Long before it was considered a sport, hunting was a necessity. For a man living out in the country, it was like breathing; he began learning about it before he was old enough to understand what it was he was doing, or why. (Let us not forget that many Southern women were good hunters, too.) There were professional hunters, who brought their bounty to market, much like farmers. Then, with an increase in leisure time and wealth, elaborate hunts were staged that resembled African safaris more than coon hunts in Southern hill country.

If you're a Southerner and you've never been fishing, it could only be because you come from one of the few dry landlocked areas in our region. If you're a fisherman and you've never told a tall tale about your catch, it must be because you had witnesses. The invention of photography meant that fishermen could record their more spectacular catches —as was the case with the Texan and his magnificent alligator gar (top right corner, circa 1920). Folks near the coast take plenty of red snapper, flounder, shrimp, and crabs, while bass, bream, and catfish are the hoped-for catches in inland streams and ponds.

By buggy, bike, and foot, visitors
are drawn to a happening further
up the shore at Daytona Beach in 1904.
Barely a square inch of skin is
exposed to the Florida sun.

No one would pretend that most Southern men were good cooks. The society was too rigidly organized along traditional lines to allow them much practice, except in the case of kitchen servants. But there were certain times when it was a man's turn; usually, the occasion was a hunting trip or other gathering of men, and it often took place outdoors. No doubt the stews simmering in those big pots were hearty, fragrant, and rib-sticking.

Brunswick stew is probably the good stuff simmering in the iron vats, above. The outdoor occasion, taking place in Virginia in the 1930s, is not identified. Above right: Fire captains Ernest and Kuhlmann stir up a "deep sea mulligan stew" at the Central Fire Station in San Antonio, Texas (circa 1925).

At the Tuckahoe Plantation, in Goochland County on Virginia's James River, a waiter rushes hot food from the kitchen to the main house along the "Battercake Express." Below: Well-tended by male chefs, dinner-on-the-grounds—a summer pleasure all over the South—under way at San Pedro Park, Texas, in the 1920s.

They say that in some of the coastal cities such as Charleston and New Orleans, vendors would stroll through the streets in the early morning, singing a song as advertisement. But most Southerners' experience with fresh fruits and vegetables came either from their own labor in a garden, from vendors who would stack their wares-of-the-moment on a town street corner, or from a roadside stand like the one in Georgia, at right.

A strawberry vendor and browsers in
New Orleans (upper left, 1890s).
Left: The iceman waiteth, Harlingen,
Texas, 1939. Above: A farm stand in
Chatham County, Georgia (circa 1940).
Right: To show the superiority of a
new potato bin introduced in 1920 by
Southern Wood Products, Mrs. Regnell
of Louisville demonstrates easy
access to spuds in the new design.
The potato barrel, in which a
grocer is groping, has clearly been
assigned the role of has-bin.

Southern hospitality invariably takes a comestible turn and Southern cookery ranges from concoction to alchemy. Situations promising good things to eat are shown here clockwise from upper left: Steaming crabs at Pope's Creek, Maryland, 1960s; preparing a picnic supper at St. Thomas Church in Bardstown, Kentucky, 1940; a proud cook at Tuckahoe Plantation, Virginia (undated); frozen desserts under way in Roanoke County, Virginia, 1931; 4-H demonstration at Sandersville High School, Georgia, 1920; child working a churn in Randolph County, North Carolina, 1939; the Scharer family peeling peaches in Roane County, Tennessee, 1974; Mr. and Mrs. Feggen Jones of Zebulon, North Carolina, 1942; contestant in the World Champion Jambalaya Contest at Gonzales, Louisiana, 1974; Mrs. H. W. Place in her kitchen at Green Spring, Virginia, in 1947.

W ell into this century, the breads, biscuits, and cakes eaten by most
Southerners were baked at home. Waking to rich smells coming
from a warm kitchen is the stuff of memory for a good number of us.
Above, herself as solid as any granite sphinx, a Louisville
baker's head cover advertises Ballard's Obelisk Flour (1921). Gradually,
mixes pioneered by food innovators such as Duncan Hines of
Bowling Green, Kentucky (left, 1946), shortened the process of making
things from scratch. But to this day, in households across the South,
store-bought is, at best, reluctantly accepted in place of homemade.

John Wrobble, chief baker at Fort Sam Houston, stands by his product (early 1900s). At right, John Mayr's bakery and family, Baltimore, 1909. Below, a home economics class in Rabun Gap, Georgia, 1905.

My grandmother worked all summer long, as the different fruits and vegetables came in, carefully canning and preserving them. For some reason, it always involved staying up late at night. There was a pantry absolutely full of food in mason jars. Everything that could be grown was put up for the winter. (My personal favorites were the spiced peaches.) But the wonderful tastes and aromas that came out of those jars when you opened them up in February were just the side benefits of an economic necessity. There was no twenty-four-hour supermarket just down the road, and people couldn't have afforded to buy anything there, anyway. If they didn't grow it themselves in the summer and put it up in those glass jars, they simply didn't have it.

Opposite: A mountain woman paring apples in Appalachia (1930s). Above: An impressive display of preserves, Pulaski County, Arkansas (1931). Below: A demonstration by an extension agent in Montgomery County, Alabama (1920s).

A fearless six-footer from Kentucky, Carrie Nation had no sense of humor about whiskey. After marriage to a drunkard, a penchant for smashing saloons with her trusty ax made legend of her eccentricities at the turn of the century.

Below: A gathering of the Cow Horn Club in Richmond County, Georgia, 1901. Members were Civil War vets called to meet by the blast of a cow horn. Agenda: mint juleps.

Towels attached to this magnificent Louisiana bar served as communal napkins after nickel beer and free lunch (circa 1905). Below: Lawmen of Emanuel County, Georgia, bring in a captured still (circa 1920).

Ah, Demon Rum! It brought hilarity to many an evening and the breakup (or, at best, the threatened breakup) of many a marriage. A bad marriage to a presumably dedicated tippler sent Carrie Nation out with her ax, and that very forbidding image was enough to strike fear, if not abstinence, in the heart of any saloonkeeper. There was always a secret Southern fondness for the man who made his own; most people, if they saw an old wagon trundling along with too many sacks of corn, just smiled and looked the other way. Today the moonshiner is the stuff of legend, and he's an archetype of the way everyone else pictures the South. Just as real were the elegant places in New Orleans where a man could stand by an elegant bar and have himself a Sazerac, an eye-rolling cocktail as potent, in its own way, as "shine."

A snappily bow-tied Corpus Christi soda jerk,
hat perched at a rakish angle,
tosses together a house specialty (1939).

They are mostly gone now, the soda fountains. The drugstore of today sells everything from prescriptions to beach balls, but try to find an egg cream in one and you'll be disappointed. On a hot summer day, the darkness and whirring fans brought relief, while the tile underfoot was delicious on street-scalded toes. A heavenly, sweet-sweet aroma rose from those rows of bottles, the soaps, the potions, the cigars in their glass case. Soda jerking was the first skill learned by many a Southern boy, and at first it seemed a wonderful job—all those rich concoctions to stir up (and sample), all the girls in town coming by for cherry Cokes. But the soda jerk quickly learned to unlove the taste of a sundae, and found out that the girls hadn't come in to meet him, after all.

Markle's soda fountain was a popular hangout in Auburn,
Alabama. In 1946, a Coke or root beer cost a nickel,
a limeade ten cents, a milk shake fifteen. Hunger could be
allayed with a foot-long hot dog that cost a dime.

Not only teenagers and college kids sought refreshment at the soda fountain. The grown-up Richmond customers below were photographed (circa 1910) at Miller's Drug Store. President Truman, in his memoirs, recalls working as a clerk in a pharmacy at which, on the way home to Sunday dinner after church, citizens of Independence would stop by for a nip of "special medicine." At left, a turn-of-the-century Houston interior.

There was a store on the highway near my grandparents' place, and we would go there sometimes for a treat. The treat for me was always the same—an Orange Crush in a ribbed bottle. Actually, it's hard to imagine a Southern summer day without a bottle of something cold and sweet. Soft drinks were social events—like the moment at right, captured by Dorothea Lange.

Jo-Carroll Dennison
1942, Tyler, Tex.

Venus Ramey
1944, Washington, D.C.

Yolande Betbeze
1951, Mobile, Ala.

Neva Jane Langley
1953, Macon, Geo.

Marian McKnight
1957, Manning, S.C.

Mary Ann Mobley
1959, Brandon, Miss.

Maria Beale Fle
1962, Asheville,

Beauty pageants have provided for young Southern women pretty much what football has provided for young Southern men—the thrill of competition. Happily for the uncrowned beauty queen, the agony of defeat carries no greater pain than a broken heart.

That seems to be small consolation to sulky Miss Lake Charles in the picture at left, taken at a Texas pageant in the 1920s. The beauties at right are competing for the title of Miss Virginia Beach, 1926.

Miss America is the title most coveted by aspiring queens. (Early on, the Miss America pageant resembled the 1924 contest in Galveston, Texas, pictured at bottom.) Some of the dazzling Southern winners of the Miss America crown are shown below. Determined Yolande Betbeze refused to pose in a Catalina swimsuit, which led the furious sponsor to initiate the Miss Universe pageant.

In recent years, Mississippi has claimed a generous share of crowns. "Ole Miss" Chi Omega sisters Mary Ann Mobley and Lynda Lee Mead caused a furor by winning the Miss America title successively in 1959 and 1960. Cheryl Prewitt added another tiara to the Mississippi collection in 1980. Since then, no contestant from that state has failed to make the finals in the national pageant.

lis Ann George
, Denton, Tex.

Kylene Baker
1979, Galax, Vir.

Susan Akin
1986, Meridian, Miss.

The phrase "Southern belle" conjures up the image of a woman for whom beauty is the requisite asset and intelligence an unlikely accident. The image is an illusion. For fifteen-year-old Eliza Ridgely, the European pedal harp was more than an artist's prop—it was a symbol of the cultural background of a lady of her class. In our own time, the Hollywood dream factory turned another teenager, Linda Darnell, into a leading lady and asked of her only ravishing beauty, a ready smile, and good posture. Her witty, perceptive performance in *A Letter to Three Wives* stunned studio moguls and delighted movie audiences. Nancy Langhorne Astor enlivened the British House of Commons by conducting a running feud with Winston Churchill. Equally difficult to categorize was Zelda Fitzgerald, whose literary gifts weren't fully appreciated until after her death.

Other ladies of differing styles and eras are pictured here—a small gallery drawn from a sparkling sisterhood.

Far left: Baltimore's Eliza Ridgely was fifteen when Thomas Sully painted her portrait in 1818.

Left: Virginian Lady Nancy Langhorne Astor was the first woman member of British Parliament.

Below left: Wallis Warfield Simpson, several years before Edward VIII gave up the crown of England to marry her.

Above: Forties film star, Linda Darnell of Texas.

Below: Mrs. J. E. Glayzer and her sister Mrs. P. C. Jefferson sport the latest hairstyle in 1929.

Above left: Zelda Sayre Fitzgerald practicing her pout.

Above: Baltimore's Ellen Ward Gilmor, as painted by William Edward West.

Left: Emily Post, also of Baltimore, published her soon-to-be-famous book on etiquette in 1922.

Below left: Elizabeth Jaquelin's portrait was painted in Jamestown in 1722.

Below: A bevy of Dallas belles, circa 1900.

William Byrd II (above, circa 1720) is the forebear of Governor Harry Byrd and Senator-to-be Harry, Jr. (the two younger men pictured at right, circa 1926). Below, Kentucky senator Ephraim Foster in a family portrait painted by Ralph Eleazer Whiteside Earl, 1820s.

Another famous father-son combination: Louisiana's Huey and Russell Long (below, circa 1935). Tobacco magnate R. J. Reynolds (at left with family, circa 1914) endowed Wake Forest University. The Hogg family (below left, circa 1895) brought reforms to Texas.

Many early immigrants fled Europe to escape the consequences of the idea that a man should be king simply because he was born to a king. America was supposed to be a refuge from the concept of nobility. But the very people who established our nation were themselves members of great and powerful families, and in many cases their descendants hold powerful offices today. William Byrd, founder of Richmond and a quintessential Virginia aristocrat, knew that "good" marriages were essential to establishing a lineage. He wrote to a prospective wife: "If you cou'd look into my heart, you'd beleive [sic] that I love you without any mean Regard to your Fortune; I bless my Stars my circumstances are not so low, nor my Avarice so high as to require it." Today, one of Byrd's descendants is a very powerful man in the U.S. Senate. The Reynolds family built a fortune on tobacco, and members of the clan still hold sway in North Carolina. Other great families rose from much humbler beginnings on the force of personality. Huey Long got Louisiana to love him by proclaiming "Every Man a King," but when it came time for his sons to move into positions of power, they were regarded as crown princes.

The old crafts are not dying out. There are just as many people today who know how to repair a harness as there were; horses aren't being used to pull plows anymore, but there's still a need for harness making and blacksmithing. We have such an interest in our past. You can't be a potter without learning how the old potters did it. Quilting is seeing an enormous resurgence right now. There's many a young Southern woman learning from the old women how to make quilts, and adding her own ability to it, so they don't all look like the old Star of Bethlehem quilts. But they're done with great skill and beauty—and will be heirlooms someday.

These people are the record keepers, without whom this book would not have been possible. They are artists and photographers, each emboldened by what he saw of the South, each with his own gift, his own particular viewpoint. It is from their works that we form our images of a vanishing South. Some, such as Edward Valentine and Rembrandt Peale, were the portraitists of their time. They portrayed the struggles of a nation, as written in the faces of its leaders. Some, such as the incomparable John James Audubon, were devoted to capturing the natural world in its glory. He intuitively sensed that these things, too, would pass. Then there were the naive artists, fresh and unformed as the landscape itself, who painted what they saw, or what they remembered. Typically, George Caleb Bingham is remembered more for giving us the teeming texture of a courthouse at election time than for his contributions to politics.

Far above: Mattie Lou O'Kelley of Mayesville, Georgia, took up painting at the age of sixty.

Above: Sculptor Edward Valentine of Richmond works on a statue of Robert E. Lee.

Above right: Robert E. Lee, Jr., poses for Valentine as his father's stand-in.

Left: Texas sculptor Elisabet Ney, whose busts of Sam Houston and Stephen Austin are in the State Capitol.

Right: John James Audubon drew heavily on his travels in the South for his Birds of America.

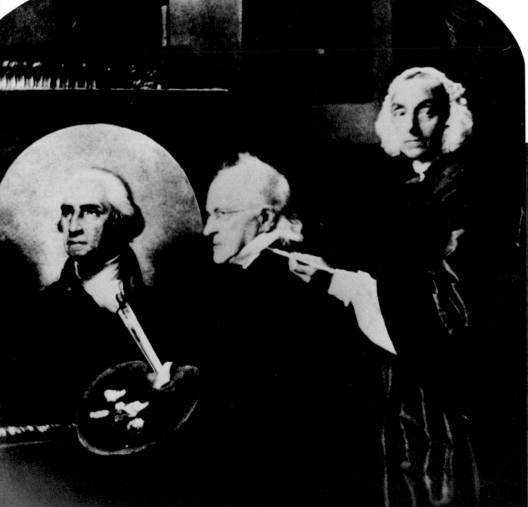

Above: The County Election *by George Caleb Bingham, circa 1851, was inspired by Bingham's unsuccessful campaign for the Missouri legislature. He won a subsequent election.*

Below: A self-portrait of Washington Allston, 1805.

Left: Rembrandt Peale, one of the famous painting Peales, with his wife, Harriet, at work on a portrait of Washington, circa 1859. The photograph was taken by Peale's nephew Coleman Sellers.

Left: A hand-cranked camera records a birthday party in 1923.

Right: A self-portrait by Elias Marken Recher, who specialized in stereoscopic images of Hagerstown, Maryland, in the mid-nineteenth century.

Below right: Photographer, barber and real estate agent Charles Petter snaps self-portrait in Louise, Texas, circa 1917.

Above: Photographer O. V. Hunt is hoist with his own tripod to get a better shot of Birmingham in 1913.

Above right: An early Texas photographer. His car door says it all.

Right: Frank Schleuter of Houston, some of whose work appears in this book.

The subject comes to the studio: Mary Burkes Via sits before a painted capitol in Richmond, below, early 1950s. At right, John Markow and crew put to sea in Galveston, 1928.

Right: Eugene Omar Goldbeck of San Antonio started working as a photographer after World War I. In 1967, he gave more than sixty thousand of his prints and negatives to the University of Texas.

Below: Frances Benjamin Johnston (right of center) ran a tintype booth at a Virginia fair in May of 1903. A highly independent woman, Frances Johnston was one of the country's first photojournalists.

It was the invention of the camera that gave a new way of seeing to the masses. The earliest rage was, of course, to have a portrait taken of yourself—then an uncomfortable proposition. A neck brace kept your head motionless during the long exposure time. But as technology improved, so did the pictures. Photographers turned their eyes to the world around them, to the landscapes and cityscapes and oddities and celebrations. E. O. Goldbeck circled the globe nine times with his panoramic camera, capturing wide swaths of reality with little artistic pretense—just like a tourist with a Kodak. That's what makes these photographs so valuable: they reflect the photographer's unvarnished vision of life.

THREE

I don't know why Southerners are, in general, so much better at telling stories than anyone else. We love to talk, and to hear good talk; which we love most depends on the person.

Northerners had substitute entertainments for talk. The city offered what Steinbeck called "the gift of anonymity." You could come to New York and vanish into whatever pursuit you wanted; I suspect Southerners have gone North to get away from the nosiness, the incessant curiosity we have in the South.

I was in North Carolina recently and stopped at a little country store near Durham, but out of the city. There they were: about five or six old guys, all retired from tobacco farming or working in the tobacco factories, who I judged spend every day right there. They were sitting inside, on chairs reserved for the purpose, and they just sat and talked.

One man, very old, way up in his eighties, found it difficult to walk, but he came walking down the highway. They all stood up and greeted him. His excuse for coming to the store was to buy the paper, but the store was obviously the place he spent every day, all day.

It didn't do the storekeeper much good for them to be there. They would each have maybe one Coke, and that was the sum total of their purchases for the day.

Because I came in, and one of them recognized me from television, they started talking about all the changes that had come. How it looked like the city was surely coming out their way, and land values were going up. They didn't like it much, but they all recognized it was inevitable, and accepted it.

It was raining, and they talked about how it had been so dry. And how crop prices were so low that it was hardly worth it to plant. And it looked like the government was sure going to cut off the tobacco subsidy, and after that, well, the people might as well divide up their farms and build houses, because you couldn't make any money in tobacco anymore.

There was one man in this store who never said a word, but who obviously was having a swell time.

You could find that scene at every crossroads. If you get into the mountains of Georgia, North Carolina, Virginia, Arkansas, and start talking to the mountaineers, it's pretty hard to get out. They tell wonderful yarns. The place varies, but it's the same people telling the same stories.

Texas Gladden, once described as "the finest traditional ballad singer," teaches a song to her daughter in 1937.

The cities are changing all that, I suppose. People are grabbing a sandwich at the Burger King, and living much as they do in, say, Cleveland. But if you want to know the characteristic Southerner, that wish of his to be with others, you've got to appreciate the sound of conversation.

There are those Southerners among us who took this peculiarly Southern gift of language and put it to paper. The result is some of the best writing to come from anywhere, any time—a body of literature far out of proportion to our numbers, and to the number of schools in the South.

The first Southern writer who impressed me was Thomas Wolfe. I think you must read him when you're about fifteen to fully appreciate what he's trying to say. He had in him an inexpressible longing for life; he wrote about many of the things I was feeling as a youngster, the longing for distant places, the yearning for knowledge.

I found a hunger like mine in Thomas Wolfe, and I read everything he had written. I think it might be too purple for me now. Erskine Caldwell has said he thought Wolfe suffered from "elephantiasis." Everything he wrote was huge. He was a huge man. I visited his grave, reverently.

William Faulkner was too baroque for me, and he was writing about a South I did not know. I recognize that he was a great writer and wrote about a real South that did exist, but it just didn't happen to be one I could connect with very well. I found him difficult going. But of course he must be first on everybody's list. His incredible intensity, his expression of all the Southern mythology filtered through a modern mind, changed literature forever.

When I moved to New York, I moved to Brooklyn Heights, because Truman Capote had just written an essay in the old *Holiday* magazine about that neighborhood, where he lived. He made Brooklyn Heights sound possible as a place to live. I didn't want to live on the thirtieth floor of some building. So I went to Brooklyn Heights first, and found a second-floor walk-up apartment in an old wooden house.

About the second or third day I lived there, I saw Capote, walking slowly down the street. I felt like his expatriate brother.

I think Capote wrote like an angel. He was a wonderful user of the language. His work has an eerie quality, very graceful and beautifully put. He saw things that other people did not see, which is the mark of a real writer.

I admire Eudora Welty beyond telling. I think she can't write a bad sentence. She is a masterful, wonderful writer—and although I'm afraid she may be something of an endangered species, an antique, that is also what I admire about her. I like antique writing. Everything she writes seems so true to me. Nothing seems written; it all seems simply to be told. Almost remembered. There is no artifice in her. There's not a false note in anything she has done.

I was delighted by H. L. Mencken when I came upon his famous essay, wherein he described the South as "The Sahara of the Bozart." At the time he wrote, there were great writers writing in the South, but none of them were famous yet:

"Once you have counted James Branch Cabell . . . ," he wrote, "you will not find a single Southern prose writer who can actually write. . . . But

when you come to critics, musical composers, painters, sculptors, architects and the like, you will have to give it up, for there is not even a bad one between the Potomac mud-flats and the Gulf. Nor a historian. Nor a philosopher. Nor a theologian. Nor a scientist. In all these fields the South is an awe-inspiring blank—a brother to Portugal, Serbia and Albania."

Now, I was in love with Mencken. I used to think Mencken was the best thing since sliced bread. But it hurt my feelings a little bit to read that essay. Of course, among Southerners who could read, it ignited much indignation. They couldn't understand: every little town at the time had its own little lady poet. What was he talking about?

I recognized that it was overwritten—as was everything that Mencken ever wrote—but it had large elements of truth in it. He wrote it in 1920, when it had a good deal more truth than it does now.

I think of that essay from time to time, now, when I'm in North Carolina at the School of the Arts, with its multimillion-dollar auditorium, or in Charleston at the Spoleto Festival, or when I hear about the fabulous new theater being built for the Alabama Shakespeare Festival in Montgomery. It seems now that every little town in the South has its own symphony, its own arts society. There's a great new art museum, the High, in Atlanta.

In many ways, there's more ferment in the arts in the South today than there is in any part of the country. Many of these institutions date from about the time Mencken wrote his essay, so I guess he could say his words did sting.

But he'd have to take it all back, if he could see the South of today. I don't see creative juices bubbling so merrily anywhere else today.

One of the most emphatic ways a Southerner expresses himself is through music, and most American music has Southern origins, from Sacred Harp singing to gospel to bluegrass to country to the blues.

Country music certainly is a kind of religion. It binds together those who live it. Country music is a family. People care deeply about the songs and the singers, and assume the singers also care about them.

Of course our folk music has its basis in the old Scottish ballads—and I will admit that I love to hear a mountain fiddle playing while somebody's singing an old ballad. I like the banjo tunes better than the Nashville sound, but you can hear the mountains even in the whanging of an electric guitar. These sad tales about the unfairness of life are to whites what the blues were to blacks.

Once in a while you'll hear a funny novelty tune, but the really popular ones are always sad, and they have the same basic theme: "My baby's left me."

Troubles and hard times give rise to our folk music. All the old English and Scottish ballads are about tragedies so awful that they're worth remembering: a boy who died for love, a woman who gave her life for her man. Blues, too, and jazz and gospel music, all came out of sadness and poverty. If everybody in the South had been like Cole Porter, we wouldn't have any music to call our own.

I'm much impressed by the revival of the old arts and handcrafts throughout the South today. Everywhere you go there's a young

Georgia's Fiddlin' John Carson (left), our first country recording star, and Uncle Am Stuart, Tennessee's champion fiddler, at a 1925 competition.

*Classroom of a
rural mountain school,
Breathitt County
in eastern Kentucky,
1940.*

blacksmith studying beside an old one, learning how to make a certain curve in a gate. There are just as many people today who know how to repair a harness as ever there were, because there are just as many horses, in places like Lexington, Kentucky, and Ocala, Florida. They're not being used to pull plows anymore, but there's still a need for harness making and blacksmithing, and many of our young people retain an interest in the past.

A lot of the young dropouts of the sixties, seeking to avoid the lockstep of the cities, went out and became farmers, so they had to learn farmers' skills. Or they became potters, and you can't become a potter without learning how the old potters did it.

Quilting is having an enormous resurgence right now. There's many a young Southern woman learning from the old women how to make quilts, and adding her own ideas, so her quilts don't all follow the old Star of Bethlehem patterns. But they're done with great skill and beauty, and they're going to be heirlooms, some of them.

There are more carvers and whittlers. Taking a pocketknife and making something has always been with us, of course, and you don't have to make anything more than a pile of shavings to be reckoned a Southern whittler. But I remember two or three skillful carvers from my youth, and if you visit the Eastern Shore of Maryland today, you find many a rural Rodin at work on shorebirds and decoys.

There are youngsters interested in dowsing, the old art of searching for water with a forked stick. I've never known for sure whether it's art or artifice.

And there are still people shooting balls of mistletoe out of the tops of trees, and selling it so people can get their kisses at Christmas. Good shooting with a shotgun is still a much-admired ability, as it always has been in the South.

I was brought up in a family that truly believed in education. My mother, as I've said, became a schoolteacher, and her two sisters, like their mother before them. Teaching was more than a job to them; they wanted to make life better for the youngsters they taught.

When I went to the University of North Carolina, any white boy who had graduated from a high school in the state could go. That school at that time was crowded with country youth whose parents were unbelievably proud of them for being in college. That could lead to anything—a law degree, a medical degree!

I think education meant more to Southerners than to others. We were surely the poorest educated of all the regions, mainly because we were the poorest. Most Southern states felt they couldn't afford to pay teachers well, and they couldn't afford to build big beautiful schools.

In North Carolina there was a succession of what were termed "good-schools governors"—men who preached how much we had to sacrifice to make our schools better. (These were as opposed to the "roads governors," who were a different bunch altogether.) A lot of people got elected on that platform—"Our schools are rated forty-fourth in the nation, and we are sacrificing the future of our children." That rang a bell.

I suspect that education was prized in the South for one reason. The

N.L. Stanton

J.I. Martin

F.E. Walker

J.A. Douglas

W.G. Wallace

F.J. Gottrel

A.B. Smith
Treasurer

E.W. Stewart

A.E. Hayes

N.M. Church
Secretary

R.C. Brooks, Jr.
Vice President

L.C. Mitchell

A.D. McGowan
President

Willie M. Stewart

N.H. Dixon
Business Manager

"WE FINISH
TO BEGIN"

M.L. Mangham
Recording Secretary

A.M. Thomas

V.M. Pelt

H.L. Jackson

P.J. Moore

C.L. Gilmore

NATCHEZ COLLEGE

Class of 1926-1927

parents saw how useful an education would have been to them. So beyond a doubt, and especially among certain black families, education took on an importance beyond the normal proportions. I can think of many families with poorly educated parents who were willing to sacrifice anything to get their children an education.

In Mississippi, I met a poor family that was made up entirely of strivers. The man owned a mule, and he decided it would be well to have another mule, so he bought the other mule on time, couldn't make the payments, and ended up losing both mules. It was bad. They had nothing.

About that time, their oldest son, who had somehow finished high school, announced he wanted to go to college. His father hitched a borrowed mule to the wagon and drove into town to borrow two dollars from his wife's sister, to give his son the bus fare to the college town. That was all they could give him.

The boy went off, worked his way through school, and by working summers made a little money to get his younger brother started.

In the end, there were eight of them who went to college. Most of them got master's degrees. One of them became head of the economics department at Howard University, another is a Baptist minister, and a third is head nutritionist at a big hospital in Kansas City. They all became very successful people—all outside of Mississippi, I'm sorry to have to say—but they all made it.

It defies the imagination that they could have done that, coming from such beginnings. Don't tell me that anything is impossible.

They decided they needed a little Negro school in Tuskegee, Alabama, and they sent a telegram to the principal of the Hampton Institute in Virginia, saying, "Do you have anyone there who could come down and start it?" And he wired them back, saying, "The only man I can suggest is one Mr. Booker Washington." He listed Washington's qualifications, which wouldn't sound like much today.

I've seen a copy of the telegram sent back by the people in Tuskegee. It says: "Booker T. Washington will suit us."

And he did.

Washington went down there, and went around on a horse to all the black farms. He rode everywhere that he could ride in a day, and announced in person to them that he was starting a school, and that they would have to build it themselves. (The first thing they were going to teach was bricklaying.)

The students built the school, and went to it, and the rest is history. George Washington Carver came there to begin the peanut revolution.

I've spent some time in Tuskegee, and to this day it has the feeling of a school that was built by hungry minds. It is the supreme example of the Southern hunger for education, the understanding that without it we were not going to get anywhere, and an example of the sacrifices that people were willing to make.

Go there, as I did, and spend a day in the veterinary medicine class, and you'll find an absolute seriousness of purpose that you don't find at, say, the University of Georgia or Chapel Hill. The students are there for a reason, and they know the reason.

What a blessing it has been for the South, to improve relations between the races. It has been the salvation of the South. For one thing, we're keeping in the South now many of our best people, black and white. You don't have to move to New York anymore to make good. Andrew Young can be elected mayor of the largest city in the South. It's not just mayor, either, it's spread all through life. Black or white, you can find a good company to work for, and you can get to be vice president, and you don't have to leave Knoxville.

I saw the end of the racial troubles as a reporter. I was down in Arkansas during Little Rock's agony, and the businesspeople solved that. It was a revelation to me that it was the chamber of commerce types who said, "Look, our businesses are being destroyed, and so is our city. Little Rock has become a bad word. We can't have this."

Orval Faubus yielded to those men, as he wouldn't have yielded to anyone else. He decided that he'd have to do something that had never been done before: start talking to the black people.

Once in a while a white preacher would get up the courage to say, "Remember that there is a mandate here to treat others as you would wish to be treated." The South solved its problems from the inside out. We've found our own solutions. I don't believe, as do some historians, that economics determines history. But I saw that business was the powerful impulse, in city after city, for ending unjust practices.

Of course, it wasn't all money. Simple decency had a lot to do with it.

I think there is something Southern about this ability to adjust. Southern whites say they are accustomed to black people, as blacks are to whites; we all grew up together. That is a cliché with much simple truth to it. Black people were never threatening, except to the slack-jawed, ignorant poor whites of the Ku Klux Klan mentality. In the old days, Northerners felt more threatened by black people—after all, in the North a black man might have had a chance to take a white man's job.

As a kid, I never questioned segregation; it was just the rules. I was a little embarrassed on the buses when there were black people standing so that white people could sit down. I realized that was wrong. But I lived with segregation in an attitude of childish acceptance.

By the time I started college, I began to think of it as stupid, and after a while, I saw that it was also evil. As a young reporter, I was on one of the Freedom Rides, going from Alabama to Mississippi on the bus. It was really and truly frightening, even though I was on the second ride, which had a lot more reporters on it than civil rights workers. It was like going into combat. I was ready for violence. Even though there were National Guard troops escorting the bus, I felt afraid. I wasn't quite sure whose side they were on.

I'm not so sentimental that I tear up easily. But I do remember that a few days after John Kennedy's assassination, I was driving from San Francisco down to Sunnyvale, California. Lyndon Johnson was making his first speech to the Congress as President. Remember that the Civil Rights Bill had been in trouble, and it didn't appear that it was going to pass.

And Johnson said: "No memorial oration or eulogy could more eloquently honor President Kennedy's memory than the earliest possible passage of the Civil Rights Bill for which he fought so long."

Mississippi State Highway Patrolmen in formation at the State Capitol in Jackson in June 1966.

There was a burst of applause, and then Johnson went on: "We have talked long enough in this country about equal rights. We have talked for 100 years or more. It is time now to write the next chapter—and to write it in the books of law."

He couldn't quite finish that sentence for the cheering.

I had to drive off the side of the road because my eyes were so full of tears. I remember thinking, "It is a government of laws, not of men, after all, and even the worst calamity hasn't changed that."

And they did pass that law. I find myself tearing up now, remembering it. It seemed to me to be a great historic moment, something rare that expressed the goodness of the country.

I remember something that happened to me in Valdosta, Georgia, several years later. We stopped for gas. There were three guys working in the gas station: two of them black, and one of them white. And the white guy came out, filled our tank and washed the windshield—and when we paid him, he turned to the black man, gave him the money. The black man reached in his pocket and peeled off the change. He was the manager.

They were all friends there, working together. I remember thinking that I had just seen the end of a time.

Blacks and whites working together in blue-collar jobs is the most amazing thing of all. In the blink of an eye, everything is completely different. Black workers still earn less than whites, but that will change too, with the spread of education and a sense of fairness, and with laws to strengthen opportunity.

The kids today don't know how drastically everything has changed. It seems natural to them to go to school and play with children of other races. Integration has worked.

Time is not the same in the South. The clocks run slower here. People drive differently. I get impatient when I drive through Southern cities, because when the stoplight turns yellow, people actually stop. I guess in the old days there was a clock in every house that could afford one, but it wasn't used very much—only to tell when it was time to go to church, when to get the kids off to school. Even if you lived in town, life moved right along in that slow, easy rhythm. Ever been in a courthouse square at high noon? It's the absolute center of activity for most towns, where people assemble to perform the public acts of their lives. Yet nobody ever seems to be in a rush.

Harper Lee's description in *To Kill a Mockingbird* is just right: "People moved slowly then. They ambled across the square, shuffled in and out of the stores around it, took their time about everything. A day was twenty-four hours long but seemed longer. There was no hurry, for there was nowhere to go, nothing to buy and no money to buy it with, nothing to see outside the boundaries of Maycomb County."

Of course, in the towns, people found plenty of ways to prevent life from becoming monotonous. Every conceivable holiday was celebrated with a school or church pageant, a parade, a concert in the bandstand (if the town was big enough to have one), a party. Birthdays were elaborate affairs, as were weddings, christenings, funerals. The automatic response to any of these events was to prepare wonderful food, and lots of it.

When automobiles appeared in the towns, life began to change.

Things moved faster. The bigger towns and cities got streetcar lines, which picked up the pace even more. But still nothing seemed to move faster than it ought to.

Our Southern weather, and in particular our Southern summers, had contributed to the easy pace. The simple fact is that it makes little sense to move very fast in south Georgia in August. But today they're all moving fast in Atlanta. Atlanta is air-conditioned. Atlanta, Miami, Dallas, and Houston emphatically wouldn't exist without air-conditioning.

I was down at Opryland a while back. They've turned a country music radio show into a huge, complicated, multimillion-dollar amusement park which doesn't have much to do with country music, but has a lot to do with air-conditioning and the interstate highway.

The urbanization of the South has made us more like everybody else. The distinctions between the South and other regions are being slowly but surely rubbed out. Certainly the look of the cities and the interstate highways is just like the rest of the country.

It's hard, in this new, sparkling South, to tell one city skyline from another. I'm glad there are people in towns large and small who now dedicate themselves to preserving the unique features of the places they live.

New Orleans, for instance, is not a bit like Atlanta or Charlotte or Birmingham. It is our distinctive American city—the one city where you can see the past palpably before you, in the French Quarter and the Garden District. There's no other city like it.

Charleston has several blocks, down around the Battery, where you can see and feel how it must have been. When you come to a little place like St. Augustine, you get more than a hunch that we weren't settled by Englishmen only. But most evidence of what we were is gone with the wind.

There are plenty of smaller places where the past is preserved, in some cases almost intact. Fredericksburg, Virginia, looks much as it did when Robert E. Lee defended it. Washington, Louisiana, is the same way; and Oxford, Mississippi, and Milledgeville, Georgia, and countless other towns sprinkled here and there across the South.

My big-city Southern experience, as I was growing up, was confined to a couple of years in Atlanta. And for me, Atlanta was all baseball. I became an absolute baseball fanatic. I played sandlot ball every day after school. Every Saturday I went to the Atlanta Crackers ball games.

The end of the streetcar line was just over the hill from where we lived, down on Piedmont Road. You'd get on the streetcar, go downtown, and then change to the Ponce de León trolley. You got a transfer. For a nickel, then, you could ride to Ponce de León Park to see a game.

Mind you, this was very minor league baseball, since it was the early forties and all able-bodied people were off fighting the war. But that didn't matter to me. I knew every detail about every player, from having read the sports pages. During the week, I'd listen to the games on the radio.

There was a little breezeway between our garage and the house, and out there I would go, and hear every single game the Crackers played. I kept a series of notebooks, in which I took down every single play of the season.

That was the beginning of my interest in journalism, keeping those

painstaking records. I started a little neighborhood newspaper, using scratch pads my father brought home from the Social Security office. I don't suppose my life would have turned out as it has, if I hadn't had that short time in the big city.

But I keep talking about the past, and not the South that is today. Today, if a Northerner crosses the Mason-Dixon line and drives on the interstate all the way to Mississippi, he'll have a hard time immediately noticing much that is different from what he's used to. Unless he gets off on the back roads, and sees the old unpainted farm houses that survive to this day.

When someone sits down in the year 2015 to write a book about the South, they will not have much of this to remember. Their South will be the South of six-lane highways and big cities. No more mills with blue windows, no more country stores with faded Dr. Pepper signs. It will be the quiet IBM complex out there in the country. It's all around us now; you can see it happening everywhere.

There are still enormous cotton farms in the Mississippi Delta where you can smell and feel the Old South, though today they're just as likely to be catfish farms. I visited a plantation there that has been turned to the raising of catfish. This farmer has a mile or two of aerated ponds. They feed the fish with an airplane—they bank over, come down low over the ponds, and spray high-protein soybean pellets into the water. The fish come up and eat like crazy.

Every month or so a tank truck pulls up, and they pump all the live catfish out and truck them to market. It's not a bit like fishing, or even like farming, or anything I know. But it's the new agricultural South, it's changing fast, and now I can walk into the A&P in lower Manhattan and buy fresh catfish; catfish has become trendy.

There's a certain symbol in that.

On balance, you can't weep about what has happened to the South. Changes of heart have taken place. People who said "never" to the new ways are now admitting, "Well, we have a better place now because of those changes." Much poverty and sickness and ignorance have gone the way of yeoman farms and homemade country hams. The price we pay is losing some of the valuable things, too.

Writing on the eve of World War II, W.J. Cash closed his brilliant book *The Mind of the South* with this problem: "In the coming days, and probably soon, [the South] is likely to have to prove its capacity for adjustment far beyond what has been true in the past. And in that time I shall hope, as its loyal son, that its virtues will tower over and conquer its faults and have the making of the Southern world to come."

Cash was a prophet. The faults of the South are yielding to its virtues at an ever-quickening pace. Beyond a doubt, we have reached the Southern world that he envisioned.

I'll bet that in the South of the distant future, there still will be good food, good neighbors, a beautiful land, and a shared accent and outlook that mark us as brothers and sisters to one another.

I predict we'll adjust and hang on and make do, as Southerners always have done. We Southerners will keep on surviving. We know how it's done.

In Houston, the RepublicBank Center, completed in 1983, looms over San Felipe Cottage, built by immigrants in 1868.

PICTURE CREDITS

Key to credits

ADAH—*Alabama Department of Archives and History, Montgomery, Alabama*
GDAH—*Georgia Department of Archives and History*
HMRC, HPL—*Houston Metropolitan Research Center, Houston Public Library*
HNO—*The Historic New Orleans Collection*
ITC—*Institute of Texan Cultures*
LC—*Library of Congress*
MSA—*Maryland State Archives/Merrick Photographic Archives*
NA—*National Archives*
NPG—*National Portrait Gallery, Smithsonian Institution, Washington, DC*
NYPL—*The New York Public Library, Astor, Lenox and Tilden Foundations*
THG—*Thomas H. Gandy Collection, Natchez, Mississippi*
TSL—*Courtesy, Archives Division, Texas State Library*
UL—*University of Louisville Photographic Archives*
VM—*Valentine Museum, Richmond, Virginia*

1: Elizabeth Koch Collection, ITC. **2,3:** Margaret Bourke-White, Life Magazine © TIME Inc. **4:** © William A. Bake. **6:** LC. **8:** LC. **10:** UL. **12,13:** Courtesy GDAH. **14:** Copyright © 1983 by Mattie Lou O'Kelley. From her book *From the Hills of Georgia.* Reprinted by arrangement with Little, Brown & Co., Inc., in association with the Atlantic Monthy Press. **16:** Progressive Farmer. **18:** VM. **20:** NA. **22:** UL. **24:** LC. **26:** Georgia Southern Museum. **28:** Progressive Farmer. **30:** photo by Jim Smith. **32,33:** Truman: Harry S. Truman Library. A. Johnson, Taylor, Wilson, Carter: LC. Jefferson: courtesy of The New-York Historical Society. Washington: Owned jointly by the NPG and the Museum of Fine Arts, Boston. Polk, Jackson: International Museum of Photography at George Eastman House, Rochester, NY. Tyler, Monroe, Madison: NPG. L. Johnson: Lyndon Baines Johnson Library. Harrison: Metropolitan Museum of Art, Gift of I. N. Phelps Stokes, Edward S. Hawes, Alice Mary Hawes, Marion Augusta Hawes, 1937. **34,35:** Lee: Washington-Custis-Lee Collection, Washington & Lee University. Galt: © White House Historical Association; Photograph by the National Geographic Society. Pocahontas: NPG. Polk: Home of President James K. Polk. Davis: Museum of the Confederacy. Madison: courtesy of The New-York Historical Society. Washington: owned jointly by the NPG and the Museum of Fine Arts, Boston. Truman: Harry S. Truman Library. Carter, Arthur, Jackson: LC. Johnson: Lyndon Baines Johnson Library. McCardle: Andrew Johnson National Historic Site, Greenville, Tennessee. **36,37:** Dickinson, Read: LC. Chase: Maryland Historical Society. Harrison: courtesy of the President Benjamin Harrison Memorial Home, Indianapolis, Indiana. Pinckney: NPG. Carroll: Metropolitan Museum of Art, Rogers Fund, 1956. Lee: Independence National Historic Park. Walton: Yale University Art Gallery, Mabel Brady Garvan Collection. Cowpens: Captiol, State of South Carolina. **38,39:** Natives: Print Collection, NYPL. Map: Geography Map Division, LC. Sequoyah: NPG. Trail of Tears: Woolaroc Museum, Bartlesville, Oklahoma. **40,41:** The Metropolitan Museum of Art, Gift of Edgar William and Bernice Chrysler Garbisch, 1963. **42,43:** top: LC. left: Mount Vernon Ladies' Association. right: Abby Aldrich Rockefeller Folk Art Center, Williamsburg, Virginia. **44,45:** top left: Abby Aldrich Rockefeller Folk Art Center, Williamsburg, Virginia. top right: RepublicBank Corporation, Dallas. bottom left: Chicago Historical Society. bottom right: Wachovia Historical Society. **46,47:** left: Washington-Custis-Lee Collection, Washington and Lee University. right: LC. **48-49:** S. Lee, Early, Ewell, Forrest, Pickett, A. Hill, Bragg: LC. Longstreet, Johnston, Hampton, Gordon, Hood, Stuart, D. Hill: VM. Beauregard, Jackson: NA. Mosby: NPG. **50,51:** column 1, top to bottom: William Albaugh, copy courtesy National Historical Society (NHS). VM. Confederate Memorial Hall, New Orleans (CMH). William S. Powell, Chapel Hill, NC. The Bettmann Archive. column 2: Museum of the Confederacy (MC). Ronn Palm. column 3: Frank R. Johnson. Southern Historical Collection, UNC at Chapel Hill. MC. MC. column 4: Herb Peck, Jr., copy courtesy NHS. National Anthropological Archives, Smithsonian Institution. Wendell W. Lang, Jr., copy courtesy NHS. column 5: Mary Louise Tucker. LC. Ronn Palm. column 6: MC. Ms. Janet F. Taylor, copy courtesy Carroll Walker. Ronn Palm. column 7: Special Collections, Hill Memorial Library, Louisiana State University Libraries. CMH. John A. Hess, copy courtesy NHS. LC. column 8: NHS. CMH. column 9: LC. LC. column 10: LC. Herb Peck, Jr., copy courtesy NHS. NHS. column 11: Herb Peck, Jr., copy courtesy NHS. CMH. NHS. CMH. **52,53:** UL. **54,55:** left: Collection of Mr. and Mrs. Theodore Strauss, Dallas, TX. right: LC. **56:** Old Court House Museum Collection, Vicksburg, Mississippi. **57:** Musée Muncipal des Beaux-Arts, Pau, France. **58,59:** top left: LC. top right, bottom left: photo by Bruce Roberts. bottom right: photo by Dick Agnew. **60,61:** left: Courtesy, GDAH. right: VM. **62,63:** LC. **64,65:** left: LC. right: VM. **66,67:** Southern Highlands Research Center, University of North Carolina at Asheville. **68,69:** top left, top right: UL. bottom left: Photographic Archives, Vanderbilt University. bottom right: photo by Jim Smith. **70,71:** left: MSA MdHR G#1477-5826. top right: Private Collection. bottom right: NA. **72,73:** top left: ADAH. bottom left: The *San Antonio Light* Collection, copy courtesy ITC. right: Progressive Farmer. **74,75:** photo by Geoff Winningham. **76,77:** boys with livestock: Progressive Farmer. two boys: E. W. Ahlrich, copy courtesy ITC. watermelon: Old Court House Museum. Vicksburg. wheat: photo by Bruce Roberts. figs: HMRC, HPL. cows: UL. squash: HNO #1978.192.9. **78,79:** top left: MSA MdHR G#1477-5617. bottom left: Memphis Room, Memphis/Shelby County Public Library and Information Center. top right: Auburn University Archives. bottom right: Harris County Heritage Society. **80,81:** left: LC. top right: THG. bottom right: Mrs. Charles C. Bush, III, San Antonio, Texas, copy courtesy ITC. **82,83:** top left: Wharton County Historical Museum, Wharton, Texas. bottom left: Baker Barber Collection, Hendersonville, North Carolina. top right: LC. **84,85:** top left: THG. left: HNO #1974.25.19.314. right: HNO #1974.25.19.132. **86,87:** maypole: courtesy, GDAH. flag: HNO #1981.238.7. rabbits: LC. angels, stars: UL. Indians: Ernestine Edmunds Collection, San Antonio Conservation Society, copy courtesy ITC. Columbus Day: THG. fisherman: HNO #1979.246.5. cat: The *San Antonio Light* Collection, copy courtesy ITC. **88,89:** top left: photo by Bruce Roberts. right: MSA MdHR G#1477-5172. **90,91:** Atlanta Historical Society. **92,93:** left: UL. right: © Michael Disfarmer/Archive Pictures Inc. **94,95:** top row, left to right: © Michael Disfarmer/Archive Pictures, Inc. VM. THG. UL. THG. VM. second row, left to right: THG. THG. UL. THG. bottom row, left to right: photo by P. H. Polk. THG. HMRC, HPL. THG. Beatrice Clay, copy courtesy ITC. Courtesy, GDAH. **96,97:** top left: National Gallery of Art, Washington; Gift of Edgar William and Bernice Chrysler Garbisch. bottom left: The *San Antonio Light* Collection, copy courtesy ITC. top center: Martha S. Martin, San Antonio, Texas, copy courtesy ITC. bottom center: courtesy of Louisiana State Museum. right: © Michael Disfarmer/Photo Archives Inc. **98,99:** left: Courtesy, GDAH. top right: LC. **100,101:** Courtesy, GDAH. **102,103:** left, top right: LC. top left: Ulmann Collection, University of Oregon Library. **104,105:** From *From the Hills of Georgia: An Autobiography in Paintings* by Mattie Lou O'Kelley. Copyright © 1983 by Mattie Lou O'Kelley. By permission of Little, Brown & Co., Inc. in association with The Atlantic Monthly Press. **106:** courtesy of Salem Academy & College. **107:** clockwise from top right: UL. LC. UL. Courtesy, GDAH. Culver Pictures. **108,109:** left: Birmingham Public Library. top right: photo by Bruce Roberts. **110,111:** Low: Girl Scouts of the U.S.A. Davie: Independence National Historical Park Collection. Washington: NPG. Denny: University of Alabama, Tuscaloosa, Alabama. Bethune, Berry, Keller: LC. Neff: The Texas Collection, Baylor University, Waco, Texas. Wright: HNO #1981.307.11. Aden: Beatrice Masterson Richards, San Antonio, Texas, copy courtesy ITC. Carver: Photo by P. H. Polk. **112,113:** Cannon: photo by Bruce Roberts. nurses: HMRC, HPL. Mudd: Florida State Archives, Tallahassee, Florida. Reed, class, McGee: National Library of Medicine. dental clinic: courtesy of Kentucky Historical Society. Drs. Allen & Allen: courtesy Frances and Sheila Allen, Fort Worth, Texas. Cooley: HMRC, HPL. DeBakey: *Houston Chronicle*, Jan. 9, 1965, copy courtesy ITC. **114,115:** O. Henry, Agee, Hammett: Culver Pictures. Ellison: Photograph of Ralph Ellison by Jill Krementz © 1986. Glasgow: Brown Brothers. Lee: Courtesy of Harper Lee. Porter: courtesy of Paul Porter. Cable, Poe, Hughes: LC. Chopin: Bayou Folk Museum, Cloutierville, Louisiana. Faulkner: © 1978 by Jack Cofield. Dickey: Photograph of James Dickey by Jill Krementz © 1986. Welty: Photograph of Eudora Welty by Jill Krementz © 1986. **116,117:** Percy: Photograph of Walker Percy by Jill Krementz © 1986. Warren: Photograph of Robert Penn Warren by Jill Krementz © 1986. Freeman: Dementi Studio, Richmond, VA. Hurston, Wright, Harris: LC. Capote: Photograph of Truman Capote by Jill Krementz © 1986. O'Connor: John Zimmerman/Time Magazine. Buck: Brown Brothers. Twain: Dallas Historical Society. Wolfe: North Carolina Collection, UNC Library at Chapel Hill. Styron: Photograph of William Styron by Jill Krementz © 1986. **118,119:** Booth: VM. Williams, Hellman, Caldwell: Culver Pictures. Heyward: Brown Brothers. Porgy: the Lester Glassner Collection. Guinan: UPI/Bettman Newsphotos. Bankhead: Theater Collection, NYPL. McCullers: © 1971 by Ruth Orkin. Torn: UPI/Bettman Newsphotos. **120,121:** Mix, Griffith: Brown Brothers. Sheridan, Martin: Private Collection. Spacek, Gish, Dunaway, Lamour, Cotten, Dunne, Streetcar: Culver Pictures. Gone With The Wind, Hopkins, Woodward, Reynolds, Poitier, Robinson, Hardy, Powell, Autry: The Lester Glassner Collection. Coburn, Murray: The Memory Shop. Gardner: The Eric Benson Collection. **122,123:** Progressive Farmer: Progressive Farmer. Carter: Main Street Television Production Co. Murrow, Rather: CBS Photography. Mitchell: Atlanta Weekly. Murphy, Daniels: LC. Barber: National Baseball Library, Cooperstown, New York. Mencken: Culver Pictures. Dix: HNO #76.75.RL. Rice: Brown Brothers. Moyers: Channel 13, NYC. McGill: Special Collections Department, Robert W. Woodruff Library, Emory University. Brinkley: Private Collection. Leslie: Sophia Smith Collection, Smith College, Northampton, MA. Sawyer: CBS News/Mike Fuller. **124,125:** Fiddler: UL. Williams: ADAH. Armstrong, Jam Session, Smith: The Lester Glassner Collection. Gottschalk: LC. Holiday: Estate of Carl Van Vechten, Joseph Solomon, Executor, copy courtesy Beinecke Rare Book and Manuscript Library, Yale University. Akeman, Parton, Cline: courtesy of the Country Music Foundation, Inc. Presley: Michael Ochs Archives, Venice, California. Everly Brothers: Brown Brothers. **126,127:** Cash: Photo by Marty Stuart, Nashville, TN. Joplin: Michael Ochs Archives, Venice, CA. Lynn and Twitty, Carter family: courtesy of the Country Music Foundation, Inc. Cole: The Lester Glassner Collection. Drum and Bugle Corp.: UL. W. C. Handy: Estate of Carl Van Vechten, Joseph Solomon, Executor, copy courtesy Beinecke Rare Book and Manuscript Library, Yale University. Jackson, Miller: © Dennis Stock/Magnum. Cliburn: Baylor University. Nelson: © 1980 Warner Bros. Inc. All rights reserved. **128,129:** TSL #1/19-1. **131:** New York State Office of Parks, Recreation and Historic Preservation. Clermont State Historic Site, Taconic Region. **132:** photo by Bruce Roberts. **134:** VM. **136:** NA. **138:** UPI/The Bettmann Archive. **140:** UL. **142:** © 1985 by William A. Bake. **144,145:** Marshall: Boston Athenaeum. Taney: NA. Tubman: Sophia Smith Collection, Smith College, Northampton, MA. WCTU: Courtesy, GDAH. Brandeis: Culver Pictures. Calhoun, Douglass: NPG. Clay, bus station, courthouse: LC. **146,147:** Black, Breckenridge: LC. Scopes Trial: Culver Pictures. Suffragettes: Virginia Historical Society. Garner: Brown Brothers. Rayburn, Long: AP/Wide World Photos. Johnson: Lyndon Baines Johnson Library. Bilbo, Little Rock: UPI/Bettmann Newsphotos. KKK: photo by Bruce Roberts. **148,149:** Ferguson: The *San Antonio Light* Collection, copy courtesy ITC. Felton, King, Carter and King, Langston: LC. Parks, Watergate hearings: AP/Wide World Photos. Kefauver: UPI/Bettmann Newsphotos. Lunch counter: Greensboro News-Record Library, Greensboro, NC. Wallace fan: Photo by Jim Smith. Jordan: copy courtesy ITC. **150,151:** LC. **152,153:** Lewis, Clark, Boone, Fremont: NPG. Austin: courtesy of the Texas Memorial Museum. Bean: Brown Brothers. XIT ranch: XIT Museum, Dalhart, Texas. **154,155:** Houston: TSL #1/136-1. Scott: Brown Brothers. Gorgas: ADAH. Morgan: LC. Rough Riders top: TSL #1975/70-2296. bottom: Library of the Daughters of the Republic of Texas at The Alamo, San Antonio, Texas, copy courtesy ITC. **156,157:** Fort Story: Private Collection. Pershing, Hitchcock, Killie: LC. soldier: TSL #1972/115-C-4. cadets: Florida State Archives, Tallahassee, FL. Montgomery: ADAH. York: NA. parade: Tennessee State Library and Archives. **158,159:** mother, Shepherd, Stillwell, Hodges, Gerow: LC. Smith: NA. Hobby: Schlesinger Library, Radcliffe College. soldier on porch: UL. exercise class: Florida State Archives, Tallahassee, FL. Nance family: courtesy of Bob Nance. Murphy: Brown Brothers. Texas flag: UPI/Bettmann Newsphotos. MacArthur: MacArthur Memorial. Nimitz: Admiral Nimitz Center, Fredericksburg, Texas, copy courtesy ITC. **160,161:** boy: ©

Michael Disfarmer/Archive Pictures Inc. MacArthur: MacArthur Memorial. Hobson, military school: ADAH. Nimitz: The *San Antonio Light* Collection, copy courtesy ITC. Farragut: NPG. Westmoreland: U.S. Army. **162,163:** wing walkers: San Jacinto Museum of History Association, copy courtesy HMRC, HPL. Broadwick: North Carolina Department of Archives and History. parade: LC. Chennault: UPI/Bettmann Newsphotos. Yeager: Department of Defense photo. Crippen, McNair, Johnson Space Center: NASA. Fort Sam Houston: Florence Collett Ayres, San Antonio, Texas, copy courtesy ITC. launch: photo by Mike Clemmer. **164,165:** Bowie: Texas State Capitol, House Chamber, Austin, TX, copy courtesy ITC. Williams: photo by Bruce Roberts. WW II: Louis R. Lowery, Springfield, VA. Gatlin: LC. reaper: NA. McCormick: Brown Brothers. **166,167:** Lee & Natchez: LC. St. Joseph: HNO #1974.25.34.26. Enterprise: Newport News Shipbuilding. **168,169:** top: UL. right: LC. bottom: Florida State Archives, Tallahassee, FL. **170,171:** top, bottom: HMRC, HPL. right: Texas Collection, Baylor University, Waco, Texas. **172,173:** left: HNO #1974.25.13.155. top: courtesy of Bruce Roberts. bottom: NA. **174,175:** left: Birmingham Public Library. right: Center for Regional Studies, Southeastern Louisiana University. **176,177:** UL. **178,179:** left: Birmingham Public Library. right: LC. **180,181:** top left, center right: LC. bottom left: UL. top right: Charles Trefts Photograph Collection, State Historical Society of Missouri. bottom right: photo by Jim Smith. **182,183:** top: HMRC, HPL. left: UL. right: Goldbeck Collection, Harry Ransom Humanities Research Center, The University of Texas at Austin. **184,185:** Col. William R. Bradford and Ann Bradford Bell, San Antonio, Texas, copy courtesy ITC. **186,187:** Dukes: Courtesy, North Carolina Department of Archives and History. Hughes: The Memory Shop. seaplane: UPI/Bettmann Newsphotos. H. L. Hunt: Texas/Dallas History and Archives Division, Dallas Public Library. Lamar Hunt: Private Collection. Sanders: UL. Perot: photo by Shelly Katz/Black Star. Jones: Cecil Thomson Collection, San Jacinto Museum of History, courtesy HMRC, HPL. Coca-Cola: The Archives: The Coca-Cola Company. Flagler: The Henry Morrison Flagler Museum, Palm Beach, Florida. **188:** top: LC. bottom: UL. **189:** Mays: N.Y. Daily News photo. Mize, Hornsby, Walker, Dark, Appling, McCovey, Aaron, Chandler, Foxx, Cobb, Robinson, Paige, Grove, McCarver, Ott, Reynolds, Hunter, Terry, Speaker: National Baseball Library, Cooperstown, New York. Banks, Dean, Slaughter: AP. Jackson: HNO #1974.25.2.9. Ruth: NPG. **190,191:** Manning: U. of Mississippi. Cannon: Louisiana State U. Alabama team, Jordan, Perkins: U. of Alabama. Justice: Photo by Hugh Morton. Duke students, Baugh: Private Collection. Heath, Wilkinson: U. of Oklahoma. fans: © Tom Raymond, Fresh Air Photographics. Dye, Jackson, Bryant: photo by Steve

Gates. D. Walker: Southern Methodist U. Feathers: U. of Tennessee. Sugar Bowl: HNO #1979.325.6724. Robinson: Grambling State U. H. Walker, Trippi: U. of Georgia. cheerleaders: Tuskegee Institute. Blanchard: US Military Academy Archives. boys: © Michael Disfarmer/Archive Pictures Inc. Hutson: Pro Football Hall of Fame. **192:** Derby Day: photo by Geoff Gilbert. **193:** Arcaro, Cauthen, Shoemaker: Kinetic Corporation, Louisville, KY. gentlemen: Louisville Magazine. Singleton: Virginia Museum of Fine Arts, The Paul Mellon Collection. **194,195:** Southern 500 above and far right: photo by Bruce Roberts. Fair Grounds: Birmingham Public Library. Petty, Johnson and Yarborough: Courtesy, Charlotte Motor Speedway. Foyt: UPI/Bettmann Newsphotos. **196,197:** hotel: Orange County Historical Society. tennis courts: VM. golfers: Progressive Farmer. clock golf: LC. Zaharias: The *San Antonio Light* Collection, copy courtesy ITC. **198,199:** Hoffman: The *San Antonio Light* Collection, copy courtesy ITC. class: Goldbeck Collection, Harry Ransom Humanities Research Center, The University of Texas at Austin. Held: UL. Topperwein: TSL #75/70-5142. **200,201:** top left, bottom right: VM. bottom left: National Gallery of Art, Washington, Gift of Edgar William and Bernice Chrysler Garbisch. top right: photo by Nancy Churchill. **202,203:** top left: Cecil Thomson Collection, San Jacinto Museum of History, copy courtesy HMRC, HPL. top right: photo courtesy of Carroll Walker, Norfolk, VA. far right: courtesy of Kentucky Historical Society. bottom: MSA MdHR G#1477-5444. **204,205:** top row, left to right: Erik Overbey/Mobile Public Library Collection, University of South Alabama Photographic Archives. Courtesy of the Pensacola Historical Society. THG. TSL #75/70-4904. second row, left to right: MSA MdHR G#1477-5105. HNO #1974.25.31.191. Photo by Bruce Roberts. bottom row, left to right: Erik Overbey/Mobile Public Library Collection, University of South Alabama Photographic Archives. Courtesy of the Pensacola Historical Society. Courtesy of the Pensacola Historical Society. HNO #1974.25.25.82. **206,207:** LC. **208,209:** top row, left to right: Virginia State Library. The *San Antonio Light* Collection, copy courtesy ITC. VM. bottom: Goldbeck Collection, Harry Ransom Humanities Research Center, The University of Texas at Austin. **210,211:** top left: HNO #1974.25.20.170. lower left: LC. right: Courtesy, GDAH. bottom right: UL. **212,213:** top, left to right: photo by M. E. Warren. LC. VM. NA. center row, left to right: UL. Courtesy, GDAH. bottom row, left to right: HNO #1974.25.31.156. LC. Photo by Jim Smith. Southern Historical Collection, The University of North Carolina at Chapel Hill. **214,215:** top left: UL. lower left: The Proctor & Gamble Co. top right: Pioneer Flour Mills, San Antonio, Texas, copy courtesy ITC. far right: The Peale Museum, Baltimore. lower right: Courtesy, GDAH. **216,217:** left: LC. top right: NA. bottom right: Auburn University Archives.

218,219: far left: Brown Brothers. top right: Louisiana State Museum. bottom left, bottom right: Courtesy, GDAH. **220,221:** top left: LC. bottom left: Auburn University Archives. top right: Harris County Heritage Society. bottom right: VM. **222,223:** left: UL. top right, lower right: LC. **224,225:** top left: Cecil Thomson Collection, San Jacinto Museum of History, copy courtesy HMRC, HPL. top right: Private Collection. bottom: Harry Ransom Humanities Research Center, The University of Texas at Austin. Dennison, Ramey, Betbeze, Langley, McKnight, Mobley, Fletcher, George, Barker, Akin: Miss America Pageant. **226,227:** Ridgely: National Gallery of Art, Washington, Gift of Maude Monell Vetlesen. Astor: VM. Simpson: Private Collection. Darnell: The Lester Glassner Collection. twins: The *San Antonio Light* Collection, copy courtesy ITC. Fitzgerald: Zelda Sayre Fitzgerald Papers, Princeton University Library. Gilmor: Maryland Historical Society, Baltimore. Post: Private Collection. Jaquelin: Virginia Museum of Fine Arts, The Paul Mellon Collection. belles: from the Collections of the Dallas Historical Society. **228,229:** Byrd: Virginia Historical Society. Byrd family: Dementi Studio, Richmond, Va. Reynolds family: Wake Forest University. Longs: HNO #1981.205.2. Foster family: Courtesy of The Fine Arts Center/Cheekwood, Nashville, Tenn. Hogg family: Barker Texas History Center, The University of Texas at Austin. **230,231:** Richardson, loom: photo by Bruce Roberts. McCarter, whittler: Used with special permission from Berea College and the Doris Ulmann Foundation. Decker's: courtesy of Beverly S. Burbage. dulcimer: photo by Bruce Roberts. quilts: NA. **232,233:** O'Kelley: photo by Bruce Roberts. Valentine, Lee Jr.: VM. Ney: TSL #69/79-15. Audubon: Courtesy of The New-York Historical Society. Election: The Saint Louis Art Museum. Allston: The Museum of Fine Arts, Boston. Peales: Private Collection. **234,235:** Top row, left to right: VM. MSA MdHR G#1477-5187. photo by Geoff Gilbert. second row, left to right: Birmingham Public Library. HMRC, HPL. Lillian Petter Ripple, El Campo, Texas and Jim W. Ripple, San Antonio, Texas, copy courtesy ITC. LC. bottom row, left to right: HMRC, HPL. Courtesy Mary Burkes Via. HMRC, HPL. **236:** Virginia Folklore Society Archives, University of Virginia Library. **238:** Thomas Wolfe Collection, Pack Memorial Library, Asheville, North Carolina. **240:** courtesy of Charles K. Wolfe. **242:** LC. **244:** THG. **246:** photo by Flip Schulke/Black Star. **248:** Erik Overbey/Mobile Public Library Collection, University of South Alabama Photographic Archives. **250:** © 1982 by William A. Bake. **252:** © 1986 by Paul Hester.

The poetry quoted on page 70 is reprinted by permission of Louisiana State University Press from *The World Between the Eyes* by Fred Chappell. Copyright © 1963, 1964, 1966, 1969, 1970, 1971 by Fred Chappell.

ACKNOWLEDGEMENTS

I wish to express gratitude and appreciation to the many skilled professionals whose generosity, good will, and plain hard work have contributed to the realization of *Southerners.*

I am particularly grateful to Bruce Roberts, senior photographer of *Southern Living,* for his unstinting help in directing us to sources as well as in supplying us with a wealth of his own work.

I wish to extend special thanks to Leroy Bellamy of the Library of Congress; Meredith Collins of Brown Brothers, Sterling, PA; Jenni Rodda formerly with the Valentine Museum, Richmond; Pat McWhorter and Jan White of The Historic New Orleans Collection; Tom Shelton of The Institute of Texan Cultures, San Antonio; Patrick Bunyan formerly with American Heritage Publishing Co., New York; Chris Skinker of the Country Music Foundation, Nashville; Patricia Kelley of the National Baseball Hall of Fame, Cooperstown, NY; David Horvath and Barbara Crawford of the University of Louisville Photographic Archives; Mrs. Joan Gandy of the Thomas H. Gandy Collection, Natchez, MS; Carol Lee and Tom Kreneck of the Houston Public Library; Carroll Walker of Norfolk, VA; and Lester Glassner of The Lester Glassner Collection, New York.

Others to whom I am grateful are Clark Maurer of Culver Pictures, New York; Gail Miller of the Georgia Department of Archives and History, Atlanta; Grace Dinkins of the National Portrait Gallery, Washington, DC; B. J. Johnson of *Progressive Farmer;* John Scott, Montgomery, AL; Tom Cotter of the Charlotte Motor Speedway; Jessamyn E. Cartwright of the Amon Carter Museum, Fort Worth, TX; William A. Bake, Boone, NC; Barbara McCandless of the Harry Ransom Humanities Research Center, The University of Texas at Austin; Jane Keeton of the Birmingham Public Library; Dessie M. Hanbury of the Dallam-Hartley Counties Historical Association, Inc., Dalhart, TX; and Natasha Bellamy of Silver Springs, MD.

Others have contributed in unique ways. Harry and Barbara Ludlow of Bridgehampton, NY, helped in picture identification; Lilly Hollander in antique picture restoration and Al Cohen in retouching, both of New York City.

Mr. Kuralt and I are in debt to Mark Childress of Magnolia Springs, AL, for having written the vast majority of the textblocks on the picture spreads in *Southerners.* Other textblocks were written by Elizabeth Pearce and the undersigned, who also shared the task of captioning pictures.

To all those contributors to the publication of *Southerners,* named and unnamed here, many thanks.

Irwin Glusker